A Syllabus of Chinese Civilization

Prepared as one of the Companions
to Asian Studies

Wm. Theodore de Bary, Editor

A Syllabus of
Chinese Civilization

by J. Mason Gentzler

Second Edition

Columbia University Press

New York & London

1972

Portions of this work were prepared under a
contract with the U.S. Office of Education for
the production of texts to be used in
undergraduate education. The texts so
produced have been used in the Columbia
College Oriental Humanities program and
have subsequently been revised and expanded
for publication in the present form.
Copyright is claimed only in those portions
of the work not submitted in fulfillment of
the contract with the U.S. Office of Education.
The U.S. Office of Education is not the
author, owner, publisher, or proprietor of
this publication, and is not to be understood
as approving by virtue of its support
any of the statements made or views
expressed therein.

FOREWORD

This syllabus is one of a series of aids to the study of Asian civilizations prepared under the auspices of the University Committee on Oriental Studies for use in introductory courses and as a reference for general readers. It is meant to serve as a guide to essential information, bibliography, and questions of general interpretation, not as a cram book or as a substitute for reading and discussion.

Preparation of this syllabus was undertaken at the suggestion of a conference on undergraduate foreign area studies held at the Office of Education, Washington, D.C. in November of 1964. The original draft was prepared with the support of that office, and on the basis of experience in use has been revised to produce the present version. No doubt further revisions will be undertaken from time to time. To that end comments and suggestions are invited by the editors. It should be recognized, however, that a good syllabus always excludes more than it includes.

Wm. Theodore de Bary

INTRODUCTION

This syllabus has been prepared for use in introductory courses in Chinese civilization, primarily in liberal arts colleges. This is not the place to argue the merits of the civilization approach to the study of China; it is assumed that there is a need for such a syllabus at colleges that offer, or are planning to offer, general education courses in Chinese civilization. Of course, it is hoped that the syllabus will also be of some use in courses in the political or cultural history of China.

The aim of the syllabus is to provide a guide for both teacher and student, without unduly restricting the former's freedom of selection and emphasis in his lectures, and without providing the latter with a "trot" that will enable him to get through a course without any intellectual effort. Indeed, one purpose of the syllabus is to free the instructor from the necessity of pointing out in class which facts are essential and which are not. At the same time, while it is designed to remind the student which facts are important, it seeks to avoid explaining why they are important. That is left to the student's own reading and to the classroom.

Some principle of arrangement of the basic facts to be included in the syllabus was necessary. A chronological arrangement, following the traditional periodization according to dynasties, has been chosen as the best and most prevalent method of introducing the student to these facts. This is not meant to imply that this periodization is the best way to interpret the history of Chinese civilization, but merely that it is the most convenient point of departure for such an understanding. Most courses on Chinese civilization are organized chronologically, but even those instructors who prefer to lecture on a series of topics cutting across historical periods may find that a chronological outline of Chinese history will be helpful for the beginning student. The emphasis is on intellectual and institutional history, but important political events have not been excluded, and are given considerable attention in the section on Modern China.

The amount of factual information that the student should be prepared to know for examination purposes will depend on the length of the course and the preferences of the instructor. An attempt has been made to distinguish between persons of primary historical significance and persons of lesser importance by giving dates after the names of the former. It is thought that students in a semester or longer course should be able to identify any person for whom a date is given. Undoubtedly, there is a considerable degree of subjectivity or, as some would say, lack of realism, in this. Some instructors will want to delete some names, and others will want to add some. It was felt that including too many names would be preferable to giving too few, since it is easier for the instructor to decide which names to omit than it would be to decide which names to add and where to add them.

The syllabus makes no assumption about the length of the course it is designed to serve, nor is any schedule of lectures meant to be implied. It is hoped that it will prove useful in a variety of courses, whether dealing with a number of Asian civilizations, or devoting a full year to China alone. The syllabus does not attempt to prescribe how the instructor is to apportion his limited number of class hours. He may want to cover several sections of the syllabus in one lecture period, to linger for several weeks over another section, and to omit some sections altogether. For instance, Sections I to III of Traditional China may be the subject of the first meeting of the class, while a half-dozen lectures may be devoted to the civilization of T'ang or Sung China.

Similarly, the instructor is free to choose from a number of textbooks for reading assignments, each of which is described briefly at the beginning of the syllabus. The selection was made from a large number of available texts in order to offer the instructor some leeway in terms of length, coverage, and approach to suit the particular needs of his course. A combination of two of the textbooks, one for traditional China and another for modern China, along with *Sources of Chinese Tradition* has proven successful in a number of colleges. Some instructors may want to assign readings from several of the textbooks listed under Assigned Readings, but most will presumably find it more convenient to stick to one text for traditional China and one for the modern period.

The books and articles listed under Additional Readings include some of the best available works on important topics within each section. They may be used for general background reading, or as a starting point for the student doing research on a term paper. Works of general significance have been given preference over specialized monographs of limited interest. More extensive bibliographies can be found in the textbooks,* and in Charles O. Hucker's excellent *China: A Critical Bibliography* (Tucson: University of Arizona Press, 1962).

The discussion questions are designed to provide important and (it is hoped) stimulating topics for classroom discussion. The instructor may prefer to cover some of the questions in his lectures, but in most cases the students should be able to discuss the questions intelligently on the basis of the assigned readings. A few of the questions presume an acquaintance with ideas found in *East Asia: The Great Tradition* and *East Asia: The Modern Transformation,* or Karl A. Wittfogel's *Oriental Despotism.* The terminology used in these questions should indicate their special nature so that the instructor who has not assigned these works need not raise the questions in class. In general, answers to the other questions can be found through reference to *Sources of Chinese Tradition* and/or any one of the textbooks listed under Reading Assignments.

The remainder of the syllabus is self-explanatory. Maps are extremely valuable for an understanding of history, and it is regretted that various considerations precluded inserting more of them. For instance, the borders of Ming and Ch'ing China were not sufficiently different from those of the present day to justify including separate maps for these dynasties. The new edition of Albert Herrmann's *An Historical Atlas of China* (Chicago: Aldine, 1966) can be consulted for additional and more detailed maps. See also under Additional Readings on pp. 6–7. The Glossary of Terms is limited to Chinese words that appear in the syllabus. The author was tempted to venture definitions of such key concepts as feudalism, gentry, and individualism, but upon reflection concluded that silence was unquestionably the better part of wisdom in this case. The instructor is left to tackle these problems in his own way. The Pronunciation Guide is one of many attempts to describe the sounds of Mandarin Chinese to non-linguists through the medium of the Latin alphabet. Several of the textbooks contain similar guides, which it will prove beneficial to consult.

The list of sources for obtaining wall maps and atlases is short,

---

* With the exception of C. P. Fitzgerald, *China: A Short Cultural History*.

but should be adequate for most purposes. Unfortunaely, there are no satisfactory wall-size historical maps of China available at present. Other illustrative materials, such as motion pictures, can be shown during special hours or during ordinary class time. If carefully chosen and integrated with class work, they provide a valuable supplement to lectures and assigned readings, and are well worth the little additional effort and expense that such arrangements require. The demand for these materials is already great and continues to grow, so that it is necessary to make rental arrangements far in advance, sometimes as much as a year before use.

In conclusion, the author would like to thank those of his colleagues and associates who have contributed in various ways to improving this syllabus. He is solely responsible for the shortcomings that remain.

J. Mason Gentzler

Columbia University
March, 1972

CONTENTS

Traditional China

BOOKS FOR ASSIGNED READINGS

Books on Traditional China

Fitzgerald, C. P. *China: A Short Cultural History.* Third edition. New York: Praeger, 1961. Paperback, 1965. A survey of the high points of the history and culture of traditional China. Emphasis is on the principal cultural achievements of each dynasty, but political history is also covered. A good college-level text, either in whole or part.

Goodrich, L. Carrington. *A Short History of the Chinese People.* Fourth edition. New York: Harper and Row, 1969. Harper Torchbook, 1969. A standard work, unsurpassed for its wealth of facts on the material civilization of China and China's contacts with the outside world. Political and intellectual history receive much briefer treatment. More suitable for supplementary reading than as a basic text for a civilizations course.

Latourette, Kenneth Scott. *The Chinese: Their History and Culture.* Fourth edition, two volumes in one. New York: Macmillan, 1965. Long a standard text. The second half contains topical essays on selected aspects of Chinese civilization: government, religion, social life and organization, art, etc.

Reischauer, Edwin O., and John K. Fairbank. *East Asia: The Great Tradition.* Boston: Houghton Mifflin, 1960. The first volume of a two-volume history of East Asia. This is the most up-to-date text on Chinese and Japanese history. Excellent on political and social institutions, which are treated in some detail. Although political and intellectual history receive less attention, both are adequately covered. Ideal for upper-level courses, but some may find both volumes too detailed for use in introductory survey courses.

Source Readings

de Bary, Wm. Theodore, Wing-tsit Chan, and Burton Watson (eds.).
Sources of Chinese Tradition. New York: Columbia University
Press, 1960. Paperback (in two volumes), 1964. Source readings
of the most important thinkers from Confucius to Mao Tse-tung.
Intellectual history as broadly conceived, with emphasis on political and social thought. About equal space is given to writings
of philosophers and statesmen. Excellent introductory comments
to each selection. Designed for use in courses on Chinese civilization.

Chan, Wing-tsit. *A Source Book in Chinese Philosophy.* Princeton:
Princeton University Press, 1963. Paperback, 1969. Translations
of the major works of leading Chinese philosophers. More limited
in scope than *Sources of Chinese Tradition,* but containing
longer excerpts, and, in some cases, complete translations.

ABBREVIATIONS

The abbreviated titles used in the Reading Assignments section of this syllabus should require no explanation. Page numbers in all cases refer to the edition listed on pages 3–4 and 55–56 of the syllabus. The pagination of hardcover and paperback editions is identical with the exception of *Sources of Chinese Tradition,* for which two sets of page numbers are given in each assignment. The first set refers to the hardcover edition; the second to the paperback edition. The roman numeral indicates the volume number.

I. GEOGRAPHIC SETTING

A. Major geographic and political divisions of continental East Asia: China proper, Korea, Manchuria, Mongolia, Tibet, Annam; the island of Taiwan (Formosa)

B. Major geographic distinctions between north and south China
   1. Tsinling mountain range as dividing line
   2. Topography
   3. Soil; loess of north China
   4. Climate
      a. Semiarid north: limited, variable rainfall; 4–6 month growing season
      b. Subtropical south: abundant, dependable rainfall; 9–12 month growing season
   5. Vegetation and crops
      a. Dry agriculture in north: wheat, millet, kaoliang
      b. Wet farming in south: rice; tea and silk

C. Influences of geographical factors on history and society
   1. Mountain systems as natural barriers; importance of mountain passes for defense; regionalism in Chinese history
   2. Geographic isolation of China and traditional Chinese attitude toward outside world
   3. River systems: Yellow River, Huai River, Yangtze River, West River; perpetual danger of floods in north China (Yellow River as "China's Sorrow")
   4. Scarcity and concentration of arable land (ca. 11 per cent of land cultivated) ; intensive agriculture; distribution and density of population; chronic land problem throughout Chinese history

Reading Assignments
Fitzgerald, *China,* 1–10.
Latourette, *The Chinese,* 3–24.
Reischauer and Fairbank, *The Great Tradition,* 8–13; 19–27.

Additional Readings
Cressey, George. *Land of the 500 Million; A Geography of China.* New York: McGraw-Hill, 1955. The standard work on the geography of China, abundantly illustrated with well-chosen photographs, and amply provided with helpful, easy-to-read maps.
Fullard, Harold (ed.). *China in Maps.* Chicago: Denoyer-Geppert,

1968. This inexpensive 8½" x 11" booklet contains 57 color maps: historical, economic, and physical. Excellent for student use.

Herrmann, Albert. *An Historical Atlas of China.* New edition. Chicago: Aldine, 1966. The standard historical atlas in English.

Treager, T. R. *A Geography of China.* Chicago: Aldine, 1965. Paperback, 1968. More up-to-date on administrative divisions and some other items than Cressey, but less comprehensive in coverage. Useful maps.

II. CHINESE LANGUAGE

A. Written language: classical Chinese and modern colloquial Chinese (*pai-hua*) ; ideographic and phonetic script; terseness of classical style; single written language a unifying element in Chinese history; calligraphy an artistic element

B. Spoken language: uninflected; simplicity of word sounds; homonyms and tones; dialects; Mandarin Chinese

Reading Assignments

Latourette, *The Chinese,* 641–49.

Reischauer and Fairbank, *The Great Tradition,* 15–19.

Additional Readings

Chao, Yuen Ren. *Mandarin Primer.* Cambridge: Harvard University Press, 1961. A description of spoken and written Chinese is given on 3–71 by this outstanding authority on the subject.

Karlgren, Bernhard. *Sound and Symbol in Chinese.* Revised edition. Hong Kong: Hong Kong University Press, 1962. A description of both classical and modern Chinese by a leading authority; broader in scope and less detailed than Chao above.

Tsien, Tsuen-hsuin. *Written on Bamboo and Silk; The Beginnings of Chinese Books and Inscriptions.* Chicago: University of Chicago Press, 1962. A descriptive history of Chinese writing, with emphasis on writing instruments and materials rather than on the nature of the language. Illustrated.

III. RACIAL ORIGINS
A. Peking Man (400,000–350,000 B.C.) at Chou-k'ou-tien
B. Mongoloid and other types of Homo sapiens in upper cave at Chou-k'ou-tien (20,000–10,000 B.C.)
C. Peoples presently inhabiting China area: racial and linguistic classifications; physical features of Mongoloid type; Sino-Tibetan language group; Austronesian language group; Altaic language group

Reading Assignments
Fitzgerald, C. P. *China,* combined with assignment under Section I.
Latourette, *The Chinese,* 437–48.
Reischauer and Fairbank, *The Great Tradition,* 13–15.

Additional Readings
Li Chi. *The Beginnings of Chinese Civilization.* Seattle: University of Washington Press, 1957. Paperback, 1968. A good summary of the modern archaeological investigations into the origins of the Chinese people is given on 3–12.
Li, Chi. *The Formation of the Chinese People: An Anthropological Inquiry.* Cambridge: Harvard University Press, 1928. Although in need of updating, remains the best description of how the present-day Chinese people were formed from a mixture of various peoples over the centuries.

IV. PREHISTORY
A. Neolithic cultures, the archaeological evidence
  1. Neolithic cultures of north China
     a. Yang-shao, the painted pottery culture: agriculture, domesticated animals
     b. Lung-shan, the black pottery culture: villages, potter's wheel, scapulimancy
  2. Neolithic cultures in central and south China
B. Legendary history, the traditional Chinese view of the origins of civilization
  1. Fu Hsi, inventor of writing, fishing, hunting
  2. Shen Nung, inventor of agriculture, medicine
  3. Huang Ti (The Yellow Emperor), the legendary first emperor; invention of sericulture by his wife
  4. Yao and Shun: nonhereditary succession to rulership, based on merit; Yü and the taming of the floods; the beginnings of hereditary succession
  5. Hsia dynasty, the legendary first dynasty

Reading Assignments
Fitzgerald, *China*, 13–53.
Goodrich, *Short History*, 1–7.
Latourette, *The Chinese*, 26–30.
Reischauer and Fairbank, *The Great Tradition*, 32–34.

Additional Readings
Chang, Kwang-chih. *The Archaeology of Ancient China*. Revised and enlarged edition. New Haven: Yale University Press, 1968. Paperback, 1971. The most recent synthesis of the available archeological evidence is given on 18–184. Tends to be detailed and technical. Illustrated.
Watson, William. *Early Civilization of China*. New York: McGraw-Hill, 1966. Paperback, 1966. A reliable, nontechnical, illustrated survey (with excellent color plates) of Chinese civilization from the neolithic period through the Chou. The prehistoric period is covered on 11–44.

Discussion Question
1. Does legendary history have any significance independent of its accuracy as an account of historical fact? If so, what significance does it have? In the Chinese legends of the origins of civilization, what is meant by "civilization"?

V. SHANG DYNASTY, THE EARLIEST HISTORICAL PERIOD (ca. 1751–1123 B.C.)

A. China's bronze age
   1. Art and craftsmanship of Shang bronzes
   2. Problem of origins of metallurgy in China
B. Earliest writing: the oracle bones
   1. Divination by scapulimancy and earliest Chinese writing
   2. Indigenous development of Chinese written language
C. The Shang state
   1. Geographic location in north China
   2. An-yang, the capital; other cities
   3. Government
   4. Sacerdotal functions of king
   5. Agricultural life
   6. Methods of warfare; aristocratic warriors and horse-drawn chariots
D. Early religion
   1. Chief divinities
      a. Shang-ti (Lord-on-High, or Lords-on-High)
      b. T'ien (Heaven)
   2. Ancestor worship and fertility rites; animism
   3. Sacrifices

Reading Assignments
Fitzgerald, *China*, 34–53.
Goodrich, *Short History*, 7–18.
Latourette, *The Chinese*, 30–33.
Reischauer and Fairbank, *The Great Tradition*, 44–49.

Additional Readings
Chang, Kwang-chih. *The Archaeology of Ancient China*. Pp. 185–255 give an interpretive review of the available archaeological evidence, with a general description of Shang civilization on 240–55.
Cheng, Te-k'un. *Shang China*. Cambridge: W. Heffer and Sons, 1960. A specialized survey of the archaeological evidence, with a general description of Shang culture on 239–49. Richly illustrated.
Fitzgerald, *China*. Pp. 106–34 contain a discussion of Shang and Chou art that throws light on social and religious life.
Watson, William. *Early Civilization in China*. Shang and Chou civilization and art are surveyed on 45–132.

11

Discussion Questions

1. From the archaeological record of both the stone age and the bronze age, what evidence suggests indigenous origins and development of Chinese civilization? In what areas is there evidence of cultural diffusion from the outside world?
2. To what extent can valid generalizations about cultural life be drawn from the material artifacts unearthed by archaeology?

VI. CHOU DYNASTY, CHINA'S CLASSICAL AGE
(ca. 1123–256 B.C.)

A. Traditional periodization of Chou dynasty
   1. Western Chou (ca. 1123–771 B.C.)
   2. Eastern Chou (771–256 B.C., fall of last Chou king)
      a. Spring and Autumn period (722–481 B.C.)
      b. Warring States period (480–221 B.C., Ch'in unification of China)

B. Origins of Chou
   1. Geographic location of Chou people in west China
   2. Mythic origins
   3. Early relationship with Shang rulers
   4. Conquest of Shang
   5. Chou religion: cult of Heaven; the Son of Heaven

C. Western Chou
   1. Kings Wen and Wu: conquest of Shang and the Mandate of Heaven
   2. Duke of Chou, Confucius' ideal
   3. Authority of Chou kings; extent of Chou realm
   4. Nature of Chou "feudalism"; importance of kinship ties; bureaucratic elements; absence of contractual relations; similarities to "city-state"
   5. Economic organization; "well-field" system as ideal in later political thought
   6. Invasions, defeat, and shift of capital to east (771 B.C.)

D. Eastern Chou: political developments
   1. Decline of authority of Chou kings
   2. Rise of new border states: Ch'i, Chin, Ch'in, Yen, Ch'u, Wu, Yüeh
   3. Internal strife and usurpations within individual kingdoms
   4. Intensification of strife and gradual absorption of small states by larger kingdoms
   5. Interstate relations: the *pa* (hegemon) system; systems of alliances; failure of these to secure peace
   6. Appearance and rise of new classes: civilian bureaucrats, the origins of the literati; wandering political advisors; merchants
   7. Centralization of royal authority within individual kingdoms; examples of Ch'i and Ch'in; decline of hereditary office holding in central and local government; rise of

13

shih class; trend toward replacement of fiefs by commanderies *(chün)* and prefectures *(hsien)*

E. Eastern Chou: schools of thought
  1. Confucian school
    a. Confucius (551–479 B.C.)
      1) His life: teacher, scholar, compiler of classics, minor official
      2) His thought: the gentleman or noble man *(chün-tzu)* ; education and the educated man; contents of education; humanity *(jen)* ; reciprocity; importance of rites (or decorum—*li*) ; filial piety in the family and loyalty to the ruler; individual, family, and society; self-cultivation and social responsibility; government through moral example; merit vs. hereditary privilege; rectification of names
    b. Mencius (late fourth century B.C.)
      1) His life as a teacher
      2) His thought: goodness of human nature; righteousness vs. profit; the ruler and the people; Mandate of Heaven and the right of revolution; aristocracy and democracy; rulers and ruled; economic ideas and ideal state
    c. Hsün Tzu (third century B.C.)
      1) His life: teacher and official; his pupils, Han Fei Tzu and Li Ssu
      2) His thought: origin and function of rites *(li)* ; man's fulfillment in society; importance of education; the order of nature; rationalism and naturalism; human nature as evil
    d. The Confucian canon
      1) The Five Classics: *Book of History; Book of Songs; Book of Changes; Spring and Autumn Annals; Book of Rites*
      2) The Four Books: *Analects; Mencius; Great Learning; The Mean;* how and when these books became canonical
  2. Mo Tzu (fifth century B.C.)
    a. His life as teacher and political adviser
    b. His thought: criticisms of Confucians; Heaven and spirits active in human affairs; hierarchy of ability and obedience—identifying with the superior; universal love vs. filial piety; opposition to aggressive war;

14

organization of society to achieve social goals; idealism and practicality; utilitarianism; frugality; the "standard pattern"; logic and reason

3. Taoism
   a. Lao Tzu (dates unknown)
      1) Legends about his life
      2) The thought of *Lao Tzu* (*Tao Te Ching*) : the Way (*Tao*) ; criticisms of Confucian school; Nature, conventional morality, and nonaction (*wu-wei*) ; individual and society; the ideal ruler; the ideal society; the "uncarved block"
   b. Chuang Tzu (369?–286? B.C.)
      1) His life as seen in his work
      2) His thought: the individual and society; freedom and transcendence; relativity, skepticism, and mysticism
   c. *Lao Tzu* and *Chuang Tzu* as literature

4. Legalism
   a. Some Legalist thinkers and statesmen: Shang Yang (d. 330 B.C.) ; Han Fei Tzu (d. 233 B.C.) ; Li Ssu (d. 208 B.C.)
   b. Legalist thought: Confucianism as impractical; *raison d'état* vs. morality; wealth and power; utilitarianism vs. tradition; influence of Mohism (uniform standards; mobilization of society), Taoism (anti-intellectualism; relativity; non-action of ruler), Hsün Tzu (human nature as evil); universal standard of the law (*fa*); the ruler and the law; importance of agriculture; rewards and punishments; thought control

5. Other schools
   a. School of Names (Dialecticians) and the study of logic
   b. School of Yin and Yang (Naturalists) and the five elements

Reading Assignments
Fitzgerald, *China*, 54–105.
Goodrich, *Short History*, 18–30.
Latourette, *The Chinese*, 33–62.
Reischauer and Fairbank, *The Great Tradition*, 49–84.
Sources of Chinese Tradition, 3–16; I, 1–14.
   17–35; I, 15–33 (Confucius) .

36–49; I, 34–47 (Mo Tzu).

50–87; I, 48–85 (Taoism).

100–35; I, 86–121 (Mencius, Hsün Tzu, *The Great Learning* and *The Mean*).

136–50; I, 122–36 (Han Fei Tzu).

Additional Readings

Chang, Kwang-chih. *The Archaeology of Ancient China*. The most recent summary of the archaeological evidence is on 256–350.

Creel, Herrlee G. *The Birth of China*. New York: John Day, 1937. Paperback, Frederick Unger, 1961. The account of Chou civilization, on 219–380, remains the best general description to date.

Creel, Herrlee G. *Confucius: The Man and the Myth*. New York: John Day, 1949. Harper Torchbook edition, entitled *Confucius and the Chinese Way*, 1960. A well-written presentation of the life and ideas of Confucius, emphasizing the democratic strains in his thought.

Creel, Herrlee G. *The Origins of Statecraft in China*. Vol. I. *The Western Chou Empire*. Chicago: University of Chicago Press, 1970. A revisionist work which emphasizes the pervasive influence of the early Chou central government. Excellent chapters on royal government administration, military organization, feudalism, and relations with "barbarians."

Hsü, Cho-yün. *Ancient China in Transition: An Analysis of Social Mobility, 722–222 B.C.* Stanford: Stanford University Press, 1965. Paperback, 1968. The most up-to-date account of economic, social, technological, and ideological changes in the late Chou period, with emphasis on their political consequences.

Kaizuka, Shigeki. *Confucius*. Translated by Geoffrey Bownas. New York: Macmillan, 1956. A biographical approach to Confucius and his teachings, set against the background of his times.

Munro, Donald. *The Concept of Man in Early China*. Stanford: Stanford University Press, 1969. Philosophical analysis of Confucian and Taoist ideas about the nature of man, concentrating on concepts of equality.

Waley, Arthur. *Three Ways of Thought in Ancient China*. New York: Macmillan, 1939. Anchor paperback, 1956. An excellent critical discussion of Chuang Tzu, Mencius, and the Legalists, with brief comments on Mo Tzu and other schools.

Watson, Burton. *Early Chinese Literature*. New York: Columbia University Press, 1962. Paperback, 1972. An excellent survey of principal Chou and early Han works of history, philosophy, and poetry.

For other studies and translations of the classical philosophers, see Wm. Theodore de Bary and Ainslie T. Embree (eds.), *A Guide to Oriental Classics*. New York: Columbia University Press, 1964.

Discussion Questions

1. The state and religion in Chou China (cf. Medieval Europe).
2. Cities in early China (cf. Medieval European cities).
3. Feudalism in Chou China (cf. European feudalism).
4. Elitism and egalitarianism in Classical Confucianism. To what extent are the Confucians traditionalists? reformers?
5. The Confucian "gentleman" *(chün-tzu)*. The relationship between the ideal man and the ideal society in Confucianism.
6. On the surface, Confucius is idealistic, but underneath there is a hard core of realism. Discuss.
7. Is there a common denominator in the teachings of Confucius, Mencius, and Hsün Tzu?
8. The Taoist sage. The individual and society in Taoism. The ideal state of Lao Tzu.
9. The meaning of the term *Tao* in Taoism; in Confucianism. The general meaning of the term in Chinese thought.
10. The sources and origins of morality according to Confucius, Mencius, Hsün Tzu, Mo Tzu, Taoists, and Legalists. Consequences for social organization of each thinker's or school's interpretation.
11. Similarities and differences between the doctrines of the Legalists and those of Machiavelli (cf. *Arthasastra*).
12. The ideal ruler of the Confucians; of the Taoists; of Mo Tzu; of the Legalists.
13. What is the central problem of Chinese society as viewed by the classical thinkers? What do their answers have in common? How widely do their answers differ?
14. Nature and convention in Chinese social thought, Confucian, Taoist, and Legalist. Natural and artificial conventions.
15. The criticisms of Confucianism made by Mo Tzu; by the Taoists; by the Legalists. How do the criticisms of each school reflect its own theories?

VII. CH'IN DYNASTY, THE FIRST EMPIRE, 221–207 B.C.

Capital: Hsien-yang

A. Rise of the state of Ch'in
   1. Origins and location in northwest China
   2. Legalist advisers and policies and consolidation of power of the king
   3. New weapons and methods of warfare
   4. Conquest of rival kingdoms
B. Ch'in empire
   1. Shih Huang-ti, the First Emperor (reigned as emperor 221–10 B.C.)
   2. The concept of Emperor (*huang-ti*)
   3. Role of Li Ssu as chief minister
   4. Extent of Ch'in empire
   5. Autonomous kingdoms and feudal domains replaced by system of commanderies and prefectures
   6. Hereditary aristocracy replaced by bureaucracy; large scale transfer of aristocratic families to capital
   7. Land tax (in kind) and official salaries
   8. Corvée labor system and large scale public works: canals, roads, palaces, completion of the Great Wall
   9. Unification and standardization of weights, measurements, currency, orthography, laws
   10. Thought control and the burning of the books
C. Collapse of Ch'in empire
   1. Death of First Emperor
   2. Succession problem and intrigues of high ministers against sons of First Emperor; role of eunuchs; problem of concentration of power
   3. Rebellions: Ch'en She and harshness of the laws
D. Legacy of Ch'in empire
   1. Destruction of feudalism
   2. Imperial institutions
   3. Legalism after the fall of Ch'in
   4. Shih Huang-ti in later historiography

Reading Assignments
Fitzgerald, *China*, 137–57.
Goodrich, *Short History*, 31–36.
Latourette, *The Chinese*, 66–75.
Reischauer and Fairbank, *The Great Tradition*, 85–90.
Sources of Chinese Tradition, 150–58; I, 136–44.

Additional Reading

Bodde, Derk. *China's First Unifier, A Study of the Ch'in Dynasty as Seen in the Life of Li Ssu.* Leiden: E. J. Brill, 1938. Reprinted London and New York: Oxford University Press, 1967. The role of Li Ssu, the Legalist adviser of Ch'in in Shih Huang-ti, in the unification of China. Excellent survey of Ch'in policies.

Discussion Questions

1. Did the First Emperor of the Ch'in follow Legalist precepts in his political policies and personal behavior? Did his chief ministers?
2. What weaknesses in the Legalist philosophy can be seen in the way the Ch'in dynasty collapsed?
3. What doctrines of the Confucians (especially Mencius and Hsün Tzu) are illustrated by the fall of the Ch'in?

VIII. HAN DYNASTY, FORMATION OF THE IMPERIAL SYSTEM, 206 B.C.–A.D. 220

A. Political developments in the Former (Western) Han (206 B.C.–A.D. 8)

Capital: Ch'ang-an

1. Struggle for the empire after fall of Ch'in
   a. Hsiang Yü, the military genius: aristocratic background and character
   b. Liu Pang (Liu Chi), the political leader: humble origins; character; his able use of subordinates
   c. Course of struggle from collapse of Ch'in to death of Hsiang Yü
      1) Hsiang Yü's failure to capitalize on his early success
      2) Reasons for Liu Pang's victory
2. Foundation of Han rule
   a. Reign of Han Kao-tsu (Liu Pang, r. 206–195 B.C.)
      1) One of few founders of dynasties of humble origins
      2) Abolition of Ch'in laws; Han Kao-tsu's simple laws and less harsh punishments
      3) Han Kao-tsu's early contempt for Confucianism; reasons for later change in attitude
      4) Political structure of early Han: compromise between feudal system and centralized administration; enfeoffment of relatives and meritorious officials; employment of civilian bureaucrats
   b. Problems and policies in early decades of Han
      1) Invasions of non-Chinese tribes; the Hsiung-nu in the north; recurring problem of "barbarian" incursions
      2) Empress Lü and problem of child emperors; failure of Empress Lü to usurp throne for own family; woman rulers in China (Empress Lü; Empress Wu; Tz'u-hsi, the "Empress Dowager")
      3) Threat of autonomous kingdoms and problem of regionalism; elimination and reduction in size of autonomous kingdoms; Revolt of Seven Kingdoms (154 B.C.) ; trend toward growth of authority of central government; persistent strength of regionalism in Chinese history
      4) Staffing the bureaucracy; summoning "men of

ability" for government service; criteria of ability; first, rudimentary examinations of candidates for office

3. Reign of Emperor Wu (r. 140–87 B.C.), the apogee of Han power
   a. Beginning of use of reign titles and reign periods to indicate calendar time
   b. Campaigns against Hsiung-nu in north
   c. Territorial expansion: to northwest; to northeast; to southeast
   d. State monopolies in salt, iron, liquor, coinage
   e. State control and regulation of commerce
   f. Foreign trade
      1) Increased knowledge of outside world as result of search for allies vs. Hsiung-nu
      2) Silk Route and trade with Roman-Hellenistic world
      3) Nature and items of trade; relative unimportance of foreign trade
   g. Institutional developments pertaining to intellectual life
      1) Founding of National University in capital (124 B.C.)
      2) Appointment of authorities on classics as instructors
      3) Expansion of civil service system
      4) Espousal of Confucianism by state: Tung Chung-shu's memorial on Confucianism; Confucianism and Emperor Wu; Confucianism and the bureaucratic empire; Confucianism and literati class

4. Economic problems during Former Han
   a. Stress on importance of agriculture
   b. Land problem and attempts to alleviate plight of peasantry
      1) Reduction of land tax (from 1/5 to 1/30)
      2) Attempts to limit size of landholdings
   c. Inferior status of merchant class; hostility of imperial government toward independent commerce throughout Chinese history
   d. Debate on Salt and Iron (81 B.C.)
      1) Legalist arguments in favor of government economic activities: financing military defense; pro-

21

tecting people from merchants; ridicule of Confucians as impractical

2) Confucian arguments against government economic activities: opposition to offensive war; opposition to luxurious life of wealthy at expense of poor; corruption in government administration

5. Decline and fall of Former Han

a. Successors of Emperor Wu

b. Rising influence of maternal relatives of emperors

B. Wang Mang (r. A.D. 9–23)

1. Wang Mang's family connections; ministry; regency; usurpation of throne and proclamation of Hsin dynasty

2. Wang Mang as emperor: equalization schemes; nationalization of the land; attempts to stabilize economy; "ever-normal" granary; debasement of currency; revival of ideal Chou institutions; interest in texts of classics

3. Red Eyebrow Rebellion; other rebellions and groups opposed to Wang Mang

4. Reasons for Wang Mang's failure

C. Political history of Later (Eastern) Han (A.D. 25–220) Capital: Lo-yang

1. Emperor Kuang-wu (r. A.D. 25–57) and restoration of Han rule

a. Distant relative of ruling family of Former Han

b. Struggles with rivals for throne upon fall of Wang Mang

c. Restoration of imperial authority

2. Reconquest of Central Asia and reopening of trade routes

3. Weakness of later emperors

4. Groups contending for power and influence under later emperors

a. Maternal relatives of emperors

b. Local landed magnates: locus of power in provinces

c. Literati and bureaucracy

d. Eunuchs; role of eunuchs in Chinese history; palace life and necessity of eunuchs; usefulness of eunuchs as personal agents of emperors vs. maternal relatives, military leaders, bureaucracy

5. Fall of Later Han

a. Struggles between families of empresses

b. Struggles between families of empresses and eunuchs

22

c. Eunuchs' suppression of literati group (166–70)

d. Rebellions and rise of warlords; Yellow Turban Rebellion (beginning 184)

e. Massacre of eunuchs by warlord (189)

f. Struggles between warlords, rise of Ts'ao Ts'ao (d. 220) and his family

g. Destruction of Lo-yang and partition of empire

D. Structure of Han government

1. Central government

a. Emperor

b. Chief Minister

c. Three Excellencies and Nine Ministers; the empire and the imperial household

d. Censors

2. Local government

a. Kingdoms and marquisates

b. Commanderies and prefectures

3. Methods of recruiting officials

a. Imperial summoning of men of virtue and ability

b. Local recommendation: for local employment; for central government employment

c. Cooptation

d. Family connections (privilege restricted to high officials)

e. Limited role of examinations

E. Han intellectual and cultural life

1. Han Confucianism

a. Recovery of classics

b. Tung Chung-shu (179?–104? B.C.)

1) His career: teacher at National University; adviser to Emperor Wu

2) His thought: eclecticism; Confucian ethics and Yin-Yang and five elements cosmology; triad of Heaven, Earth, and Man, and key role of emperor in both natural and social order; significance of portents; Son of Heaven and Mandate of Heaven; comparison with "classical" Confucianism

c. Disputes and debates over authenticity of texts of classics; "old text" and "new text" schools

d. Extensive commentaries on classics; sterility of Confucian thought in Later Han

23

2. Han Taoism
   a. *Huai-nan Tzu:* eclecticism; non-striving of ruler; timeliness
   b. Religious Taoism
3. History writing in Han
   a. Ssu-ma Ch'ien (145?–90? B.C.)
      1) His life and character; Ssu-ma Ch'ien and his father; Ssu-ma Ch'ien and Emperor Wu
      2) *The Records of the Historian (Shih-chi)* and universal history
      3) The *Shih-chi* as literature
   b. Pan Ku (32–92 A.D.)
      1) His family; his life
      2) *History of the Former Han Dynasty (Han-shu)* and dynastic histories
   c. Importance of history writing in China
      1) Preservation of record of the past
      2) History as a guide to governing
      3) Moral lessons of history
4. Arrival of Buddhism in China
   a. Legends of how Buddhism came to China
   b. Buddhist communities in China during Later Han
5. Han literature
   a. Rhymed prose *(fu)*: richness of imagery and exuberance of language
   b. Poetry of common people: *Nineteen Old Poems* and hardships of war and poverty

Reading Assignments
Fitzgerald, *China,* 158–229.
Goodrich, *Short History,* 36–57.
Latourette, *The Chinese,* 75–105.
Reischauer and Fairbank, *The Great Tradition,* 90–128.
Sources of Chinese Tradition, 161–99; I, 145–83 (political thought).
   200–26; I, 184–210 (philosophy and cosmology).
   227–43; I, 211–27 (economic thought).
   266–76; I, 228–38 (historical thought).

Additional Readings
Balazs, Etienne. "Political Philosophy and Social Crisis at the End of the Han Dynasty," pp. 187–225 in Etienne Balazs, *Chinese Civilization and Bureaucracy.* Translated by H. M. Wright. New

Haven: Yale University Press, 1964. Paperback, 1967. An analysis of the varying responses of contemporary thinkers to the disintegration of the Han empire. This book contains a number of excellent articles by this eminent authority.

Bielenstein, Hans. "An Interpretation of the Portents in the *Ts'ien-Han-shu*," *Bulletin of the Museum of Far Eastern Antiquities*, XXII (1950), 127–43. A discussion of the political use of portents.

Bielenstein, Hans. "*The Restoration of the Han Dynasty*," *Bulletin of the Museum of Far Eastern Antiquities*, XXVI (1954), 1–209. The best account of the rise and fall of Wang Mang, with a valuable introduction on early Chinese historiography.

Ch'ü, T'ung-tsu. *Han Social Structure*. Seattle: University of Washington Press, 1972. Analysis and interpretation of various aspects of family relations and social classes. The second half contains translations of many relevant documents.

Loewe, Michael. *Everyday Life in Early Imperial China*. New York: G. P. Putnam's Sons, 1968. Harper Perennial Library paperback, 1970. Descriptions of daily life in Han China on all levels of society, from emperor and officials to peasants and artisans.

Wang, Yü-ch'üan. "An Outline of the Central Government of the Han Dynasty," *Harvard Journal of Asiatic Studies*, XII (1949), 134–87. An analysis, in some detail, of the organs of the central government, with attention given to shifting loci of power.

Watson, Burton. *Ssu-ma Ch'ien: Grand Historian of China*. New York: Columbia University Press, 1958. The life of China's greatest historian, with a description of his work, the *Shih-chi*, and translations of selected passages.

Watson, Burton (tr.). *Records of the Grand Historian of China*. Two volumes. New York: Columbia University Press, 1961. Translations of sections of the *Shih-chi* dealing with the early Han. The story of the fall of Ch'in and the struggle between Liu Pang and Hsiang Yü is vividly told in I, 19–121.

Yü, Ying-shih. *Trade and Expansion in Han China*. Berkeley: University of California Press, 1967. A summary of existing knowledge of Chinese economic relations with the outside world during Han times.

Discussion Questions

1. To what extent does the Han represent a new stage in Chinese history?
2. In what respects was the Han state a "modern" state?
3. What Confucian teachings were embodied in the imperial insti-

tutions of Han times? Taoist teachings? Legalist teachings?

4. Within the framework of the imperial system of Han and later times, what were the advantages for the emperor of Confucianism as the official state doctrine? for the literati? for the common people? What were the disadvantages for each?   /

5. Were the governmental institutions of Imperial China based on the assumption that human nature is good? evil? some combination of both?

6. Compare Han Confucianism, as seen in the writings of Tung Chung-shu, with the Confucianism of the classical period.

7. The interpretation of the character and goals of Wang Mang: Confucian reformer or opportunistic usurper?

8. What weaknesses in the Han imperial system can be seen in the events that led to the fall of the Former Han? of the Later Han?

IX. SIX DYNASTIES, THE PERIOD OF DISUNION AND
CHALLENGES TO THE IMPERIAL SYSTEM, 220–589
A. Political developments
1. Rapid rise and fall of dynasties; period of political and
social instability
2. The Three Kingdoms (220–ca. 280) : Wei (Ts'ao family
in north China) ; Wu (south China) ; Shu Han (south-
west China)
3. Chin dynasty
a. Western Chin (265–317) ; usurpation of throne from
Ts'ao family; temporary reunification of China
b. Eastern Chin (317–420) ; loss of north China to non-
Chinese tribal peoples
4. China and the Barbarians
a. Non-Chinese peoples in north: Mongolian; Turkic
b. Invasions and establishment of non-Chinese dynasties
in north China; Northern Wei dynasty (386–ca. 535)
c. Domestic problems of barbarian emperors: traditional
tribal organization and loyalties vs. exigencies of
bureaucratic state
d. Sinification of non-Chinese peoples
1) Gradual absorption: intermarriage; effects of sed-
entary life on nomadic peoples
2) Conscious policy of some non-Chinese rulers toward own people
3) Opposition to sinification
e. Emigration of Chinese to central and south China;
economic development of Yangtze valley; Chinese
dynasties in south China
f. Failure of non-Chinese dynasties to conquer south
China, but continuing power supremacy of north
B. Social structure; centrifugal forces
1. Breakdown of central authority within states
2. Autonomy of magnates and powerful families outside
capital areas; "feudalism" in Six Dynasties period as out-
growth of power distribution during Later Han
3. System of recruiting officials for government: nine-grade
ranking system and powerful families' near monopoly of
important political offices
C. Patterns of dynastic turnover during Six Dynasties period
1. Founding of dynasty
a. Usurpation of throne by head of powerful family

        1) High minister
        2) Military leader
    b. Military conquest by rival state
  2. Attempts to consolidate power of new ruling family
    a. Vigorous first emperors
    b. Measures taken to assert authority of central government over powerful magnates
        1) Execution of opponents and potential opponents
        2) Economic measures: military colonies and self-supporting armies; setting limits to landholdings; distribution of land to taxpaying peasants
        3) Reforms in central administration
        4) Changes in methods of recruiting officials
  3. Weak successors of first emperors and rise to dominance of one or two powerful families; puppet emperors
  4. End of dynasty
D. Intellectual developments
  1. Effects of political and social instability on intellectual and literary life
    a. Dangers of political life and feeling of uncertainty
    b. Weakness of state power outside capital and relative freedom of expression and speculation
    c. Tendency toward apolitical thought
    d. Tendency in literature toward expression of private emotions
  2. Neo-Taoism
    a. "Pure Conversation" of literati
    b. Attempts to achieve long life
    c. Neo-Taoism and science
    d. Popular Taoism
  3. Coming of Buddhism to China
    a. Fundamental tenets of Buddhism: the Four Noble Truths
    b. Mahayana Buddhism: salvation for all; compassion of Bodhisattvas; faith; secular (non-monastic) Buddhism
    c. Early Buddhist missionaries in China
    d. First attempts to translate sutras
        1) Methods and difficulties
        2) Use of Taoist terms
    e. Later missionaries to China and improved translations; Kumarajiva (ca. 344–413, in China ca. 402–13)
  4. Spread of Buddhism

a. Royal patronage, especially of non-Chinese rulers in north China

b. Popularity among literati, especially in south China

c. Appeals of Buddhism: metaphysical subtlety; personal salvation in way not offered by Confucianism; aesthetic and emotional appeal; magic

d. Chinese pilgrims to India

    1) Purposes; routes; accounts of travels as historical sources

    2) Fa-hsien (voyage 399–414)

    3) Hsuan-tsang (voyage 629–45)

5. Development of principal Chinese sects

a. Derivation from Nagarjuna's Three Treatises

b. Origins in period of disunion; growth in T'ang

c. T'ien-t'ai (Jap. Tendai) philosophical Buddhism; eclecticism, attempt to classify and harmonize various schools of Buddhism; importance of Lotus Sutra; absolute known through relative and relative seen in terms of absolute; Chih-yi (531–97), the founder

d. Pure Land devotional Buddhism: the Buddha Amitabha (Ch. O-mi-t'o-fo; Jap. Amida); Amitabha's original vow; invocation of or meditation on name of Amitabha; Western Paradise; salvation for the ordinary man

e. Meditation Sect (Ch. Ch'an; Jap. Zen) and the intuitional approach to Buddhahood: emphasis on individual enlightenment rather than universal salvation; meditation and self-discipline; intuitive grasp of Ultimate Truth; sudden enlightenment; de-emphasis on scripture and doctrine; appeal to artists and intellectuals

6. Buddhism and Chinese society

a. Supremacy of state over religious community

b. Buddhist monasticism vs. Confucian social obligations

c. Buddhist view of relation between Buddhism and state; Hui-yuan's distinction between obligations of lay Buddhists and monks

d. Services to state; prayers for emperors

e. Attempts by emperors to suppress Buddhism (446; 574–77)

f. Monasteries as philanthropic institutions: hospitals, inns, refuges

E. Cultural developments
   1. Buddhist sculpture; caves at Yün-kang and Lung-men
   2. Literature
      a. Lyric poetry: personal emotions of aristocracy; nature poetry
      b. Parallel prose: triumph of form over content and emotion
      c. Literary criticism: characterization of genres; definitions of purpose of literature

Reading Assignments
Fitzgerald, *China,* 249–90.
Goodrich, *Short History,* 58–113.
Latourette, *The Chinese,* 110–33.
Reischauer and Fairbank, *The Great Tradition,* 128–53.
Sources of Chinese Tradition, 279–305; I, 239–65 (Neo-Taoism).
   306–26; I, 266–86 (Buddhism and Chinese society).
   327–73; I, 287–333 (schools of Buddhist doctrine).
   374–408; I, 334–68 (Pure Land and Ch'an).

Additional Readings
Balazs, Etienne. "Nihilistic Revolt and Mystical Escapism," pp. 226–54 in Etienne Balazs, *Chinese Civilization and Bureaucracy.* Main currents in intellectual life during the third century.
Ch'en, Kenneth. *Buddhism in China.* Princeton: Princeton University Press, 1964. Paperback, 1972. A survey of the history of Buddhism in China. Extremely useful as a reference work on Buddhism during the Six Dynasties and later periods.
Dien, Albert E. "Yen Chih-t'ui (531–591) : A Buddho-Confucian," in Arthur F. Wright (ed.), *Confucian Personalities.* Stanford: Stanford University Press, 1962. Paperback, 1969. Pp. 43–64. The life and thought of a scholar-official who was also a Buddhist.
Sickman, Laurence, and Alexander Soper. *The Art and Architecture of China.* Third edition. Baltimore: Penguin Books, 1971. Paperback version, 1971. A richly informative survey of sculpture, painting, and architecture by two authorities who convey their enthusiasm and specialized knowledge in lucid, concise prose. Abundantly illustrated in black and white.
Sullivan, Michael. *A Short History of Chinese Art.* Berkeley: University of California Press, 1967. Paperback, 1967. Artistic developments are analyzed in the context of general historical trends.

A good chronological survey of the full range of Chinese arts, from prehistory to the present. Well illustrated.

Watson, Burton. *Chinese Lyricism:* Shih *Poetry from the Second to the Twelfth Century.* New York: Columbia University Press, 1971. Paperback, 1971. An excellent survey of poetry from late Han to Sung, combining historical and biographical information with literary analysis; over 200 well-translated poems.

Wright, Arthur R. *Buddhism in Chinese History.* Stanford: Stanford University Press, 1959. Paperback, 1970. An excellent, concise interpretive history of Buddhism in China from the Han to the twentieth century.

Zurcher, E. "Buddhism in China," in Raymond Dawson (ed.), *The Legacy of China.* Oxford: Clarendon Press, 1964. Paperback, 1971. Pp. 56–79. The best brief account of Chinese Buddhism.

Zurcher, E. *The Buddhist Conquest of China: The Spread and Adaptation of Buddhism in Early Medieval China.* Two volumes. Leiden: E. J. Brill, 1959. A detailed scholarly analysis of Buddhism and Chinese society from the third to the sixth centuries. Although some chapters may be too specialized for the general reader, this work is richly informative.

Discussion Questions

1. The persistence of the ideal of a unified China during periods of disunity.
2. Periods of disunity (Six Dynasties, early twentieth century) as offering opportunities for growth, change, acceptance of new ideas.
3. What factors affected the reception of Buddhism in China?
4. The appeal of Buddhism to the rulers; to the scholar-class; to artists; to the common people. Which sects tended to appeal to each?
5. In what respects can Chinese Buddhism be considered a foreign faith? To what extent and in what ways is Chinese Buddhism typically Chinese?

X. SUI DYNASTY, AND REUNIFICATION OF THE EMPIRE, 589–618

Capitals: Ch'ang-an and Lo-yang

A. Emperor Wen (r. 589–604)
   1. Power of Yang family under Northern Chou dynasty and Emperor Wen's early career as minister
   2. Seizure of power from child emperor (581)
   3. Unification of China by military campaigns (581–89)
   4. Consolidation of power of emperor
B. Emperor Yang (r. 604–18)
   1. Archetype of evil emperor
   2. Defeats in Central Asia and Korea
   3. Dislocation of economy due to conscription for public works and military campaigns
   4. Rebellions and collapse of Sui
C. Constructive accomplishments of Sui
   1. Reunification of China
   2. Strong centralized administration
   3. Initiation of examination system
   4. Construction projects: capital cities; repair of Great Wall; construction of canal system

Reading Assignments
Goodrich, *Short History,* 114–18.
Latourette, *The Chinese,* 138–42.
Reischauer and Fairbank, *The Great Tradition,* combined with assignment under Section XI.

Additional Reading
Wright, Arthur F. "Sui Yang-ti: Personality and Stereotype," in Arthur F. Wright (ed.), *The Confucian Persuasion.* Stanford: Stanford University Press, 1960. Paperback, 1969. Pp. 47–76. An attempt to distinguish between the ruler and the image of him as a typical "evil ruler" drawn by later historians.

Discussion Question
1. Compare the Ch'in and Sui dynasties.

XI. T'ANG DYNASTY, THE GROWTH OF THE
IMPERIAL SYSTEM, 618–907
Capitals: Ch'ang-an and Lo-yang
A. Founding of T'ang and early political history
  1. Revolt of Li Yuan and Li Shih-min against Sui dynasty;
     Turkic origins of Li family
  2. Li Shih-min's coup d'etat against elder brother and suc-
     cession to throne
  3. Li Shih-min as Emperor T'ai-tsung (r. 627–49) : T'ang
     T'ai-tsung and his ministers
  4. Usurpation of Empress Wu (r. 684–705)
  5. Foreign relations during early T'ang
     a. Reconquest of Central Asia
     b. Subjection of Korea
     c. Emergence of East Asian family of nations; establish-
        ment of suzerain-vassal relationship, symbolized in
        tribute offerings
        1) Korea
        2) Japan
        3) Annam
        4) Tibet
B. Institutional foundations
  1. Political
     a. Central government
        1) The emperor and his chief ministers
        2) Imperial Secretariat (*Chung-shu-sheng*)
        3) Imperial Chancellery (*Men-hsia-sheng*)
        4) Secretariat of State Affairs (*Shang-shu-sheng*) and
           Six Boards (Ministries) : Personnel, Revenue,
           Rites, War, Justice, Public Works
     b. Censorate
        1) Admonishing the emperor
        2) Surveillance of bureaucracy
     c. Local government
        1) Provinces (circuits)
        2) Prefectures
        3) Subprefectures
     d. Methods of recruiting officials
        1) Imperial summons
        2) Examination system: *ming-ching* (degree in clas-
           sics) and *chin-shih* (degree in letters) ; specialized
           examinations

3) Expansion of examination system and changes in social structure in later T'ang

2. Economic

  a. Land distribution: the "equal-field" (*chün-t'ien*) system

    1) Origins in Northern Wei (485)

    2) Classification of lands; types of land subject to distribution under "equal-field" system

    3) Permanent land (mulberry trees for feeding silkworms) and lifetime land (for agriculture)

    4) Land apportioned and reapportioned according to: age and sex categories; density of population in district

    5) Problems of redistribution; adjustments of amount of land reapportioned according to availability of land; deterioration of "equal-field" system

    6) "Rank lands" and "office lands" for officials

  b. Tax system

    1) Population registration

    2) Tax in grain on land assigned under "equal-field" system

    3) Tax in cloth on household

    4) Corvée labor (on public works) for able-bodied males

    5) Other forms of government revenue

3. Military

  a. Militia system; relation between militia system and "equal-field" system

  b. Replacement of militia by professional soldiers and regular armies (first half of eighth century); conscription

C. Rebellion, resurgence, and decline: later political history

1. Reign of Hsuan-tsung (r. 713–55)

  a. Early years of splendor; able ministers

  b. Yang Kuei-fei, the imperial consort

  c. Factions at court

  d. Decline of Chinese influence in Central Asia; defeat by Arabs at Talas River (751)

  e. Rise of autonomous Military Governors (Regional Commanders), especially in northeast

  f. Rebellions of Military Governors: An Lu-shan and Shih Ssu-ming (755–63)

2. The empire after the rebellions

34

      a. Roles of Military Governors and non-Chinese peoples in suppression of rebellions

      b. Weakness of central government
         1) Autonomy of Military Governors
         2) Decline in registered (taxable) population and financial problem
         3) Barbarian incursions in north and west China

      c. Collapse of "equal-field" system; growth of large land-holdings (manors)

      d. Tax reforms; the Double Tax (Twice-a-year Tax) of 780; incorporation of all taxes in one, collected in summer and autumn; tax on land actually held; increase in tenancy

      e. Attempts to reassert authority of central government and new rebellions of Military Governors

      f. Temporary restoration of central authority under Hsien-tsung (r. 806–20)

      g. Rise of eunuch power
         1) Eunuchs as agents of emperors vs. Military Governors
         2) Eunuchs' influence over emperors and selection and enthronement of emperors (ninth century)

    3. End of T'ang
      a. Rebellion of Huang Ch'ao (874–84)
      b. Reappearance of powerful Military Governors
      c. Rival generals and puppet emperors
      d. Fall of T'ang and division of empire

D. Five Dynasties (907–60)
    1. Short-lived dynasties controlling limited areas
    2. Warfare between rival states
    3. Forces favoring unity
    4. Cultural developments in Five Dynasties period

E. T'ang civilization and culture
    1. Ch'ang-an, the capital: size, layout, Imperial City, markets, population
    2. Foreign trade
    3. Foreign religions in China: Zoroastrianism, Nestorian Christianity, Manicheism, Judaism, Islam
    4. Official encouragement of Taoism: association with imperial family; occasional use of Taoist classics in civil service examinations
    5. Bureau of History; dynastic histories written by government officials

6. Confucianism: government-sponsored annotated editions of classics; construction of Confucian temples throughout empire; classics and the examination system
7. Buddhism
   a. Growth and spread of Buddhism; Pure Land and Meditation sects (see p. 29, Section IX, D, 5, d and e)
   b. Confucian attacks on Buddhism; Fu Yi; Han Yü (768–824)
   c. Confucian objections to Buddhism: foreign religion; not mentioned in classics; neglect of filial piety; selfish concern for personal salvation vs. Confucian ideal of fulfillment of individual in society; state within the state; drain on manpower, land, and wealth; immorality of damaging human body (shaving head; cremation)
   d. Persecution of Buddhism (841–46); influence of Taoists on emperor; desire to expropriate wealth of monasteries and to secularize nonproductive monks and nuns; influence of Confucianism
   e. Other reasons for decline of Buddhism in China: inner decay; revitalization of Confucianism (especially in Sung dynasty)
8. Literature
   a. Great age of poetry: Wang Wei; Tu Fu; Li Po; Po Chü-yi; poetry and the examination system; Confucian themes
   b. Short stories in classical language

Reading Assignments
Fitzgerald, *China,* 293–355.
Goodrich, *Short History,* 118–42.
Latourette, *The Chinese,* 142–69.
Reischauer and Fairbank, *The Great Tradition,* 153–93.
Sources of Chinese Tradition, 411–37; I, 369–82.

Additional Readings
Fitzgerald, C. P. *Son of Heaven: A Biography of Li Shih-min, Founder of the T'ang Dynasty.* Cambridge: Cambridge University Press, 1933. A narrative history of the founding of the T'ang and the reign of the Emperor T'ai-tsung, one of the greatest emperors in Chinese history.
Fitzgerald, C. P. *The Empress Wu.* London: Cresset Press, 1956. A

sympathetic account of the only woman in Chinese history ever to assume the imperial title.

Pulleyblank, Edwin G. *The Background of the Rebellion of An Lu-shan*. Oxford: Oxford University Press, 1955. An analysis of the political and economic forces that underlay the great rebellion of 755.

Reischauer, Edwin O. (tr.). *Ennin's Diary: The Record of a Pilgrimage to China in Search of the Law*. New York: Ronald Press, 1955. The diary of a Japanese monk who traveled extensively in north China from 838 to 847, and recorded much of what he saw.

Reischauer, Edwin O. *Ennin's Travels in T'ang China*. New York: Ronald Press, 1955. A fascinating description of various aspects of life during the T'ang based on the diary of the Japanese Buddhist and supplemented from other sources.

Twitchett, D. C. *Financial Administration under the T'ang Dynasty*. Second edition. Cambridge: Cambridge University Press, 1971. A survey of economic institutions during the T'ang.

Waley, Arthur. *The Life and Times of Po Chü-i*. New York: Macmillan, 1949. An excellent biography of one of the greatest Chinese poets, whose official career spanned some of the most exciting decades of T'ang history.

A representative selection from T'ang literature can be found on pp. 217–329 of Cyril Birch (ed.), *Anthology of Chinese Literature, from Early Times to the Fourteenth Century*. New York: Grove Press, 1965. Paperback, 1967.

Discussion Questions

1. How would you define the scholar-official class (literati)?
2. Leadership and institutions of the early T'ang (militia; equal-field system; examination system; character and behavior of Emperor T'ai-tsung) in the light of Confucian ideals.
3. Buddhism and traditional Chinese society. Confucian objections to Buddhism. Reasons for the suppression of Buddhism in 841–46. Underlying causes of the decline of Buddhism in China: state persecution? incompatibility with Chinese tradition? internal decay?
4. Centrifugal and centripetal forces in T'ang China before and after the rebellion of An Lu-shan. Regionalism as a continuing force in Chinese history.
5. Cosmopolitanism vs. isolationism as exemplified in T'ang China.
6. The level of economic development of China suggested by the change to the Twice-a-year Tax.

XII. SUNG DYNASTY, POLITICAL WEAKNESS AND CULTURAL SPLENDOR, 960–1279

A. Northern Sung (960–1125)

Capital: Kaifeng

1. Usurpation of throne by General Chao K'uang-yin and founding of Sung dynasty; reunification of China by military campaigns of Emperors T'ai-tsu (r. 960–76) and T'ai-tsung (r. 976–97)
2. Organization of central government
   a. Secretariat-Chancellery (*Chung-shu men-hsia*)
   b. Finance Commission
   c. Bureau of Military Affairs (Privy Council)
   d. Effective subordination of local government and military to central government, and of central administration to emperor
3. Military weakness vs. non-Chinese kingdoms in north; tribute payments by Chinese court; policy of using barbarians to control barbarians
4. Reforms
   a. Ideological background: revival of ideals of Confucian Classics; proposals for land reform and ideal of "well-field" system; criticisms of political institutions and examination system
   b. Aims: financial; military
   c. Fan Chung-yen (989–1052) and first period of reform
   d. Role of Ou-yang Hsiu (1007–72) in reform movements
   e. Reform program of Wang An-shih (1021–86; in power 1069–76) : local sale of (in kind) tax receipts to finance local government operations; government purchase, transportation, and resale of grain and other products; state trading monopolies; graduated taxes on land; hired service system; agricultural loans to peasants; replacement of professional army by local militia; *pao-chia* system of local organization and control; practical questions on civil service examinations; Wang's versions of classics
   f. Opposition to Wang and his reforms
      1) Confucian conservatives (Ou-yang Hsiu; Ssu-ma Kuang; Su Tung-p'o) ; problem of primacy—institutional reform or moral regeneration (government by law vs. government by men) ; criticisms of Wang's character and methods

      2) Career bureaucrats; inertia of bureaucracy

      3) Large landowners

      4) Big merchants

   g. Survival of some reforms after retirement of Wang and after subsequent defeat of reform party

  5. Foreign invasions and end of Northern Sung

B. Southern Sung (1127–1279)

Capital: Hangchow

  1. Renewed large-scale movement of population to south China; density of population in south China

  2. Economic development of south China; south China as economic center of China

  3. Rich and varied life in capital

  4. Struggles at court; peace factions vs. war factions

  5. Mongol invasions and end of Sung

C. Civilization of Sung China

  1. Political aspects

    a. Increasing power of emperor over bureaucracy

    b. Increasing importance of examination system; social mobility

  2. Economic aspects

    a. Agriculture

      1) Forms of landholding: office lands; landlords and tenants; independent farmers; effects of Double Tax on landholding

      2) New types of rice (two and three crops a year)

    b. Specialization of production and expansion of inter-provincial and foreign trade; joint stock companies

    c. Trend toward money economy; increased use of paper money

    d. Growth of commercial cities; guilds

  3. Some important inventions: printing (eighth–ninth centuries); movable type (by 1030); compass (by 1119); sea-going junks; gunpowder in warfare (by 1161); refinement of porcelain techniques; abacus (by 1274)

  4. Cultural achievements: great age of painting (figure and landscape); poetry; histories and encyclopedias

  5. Spread of literacy; private academies

  6. Subordination of women; foot-binding

D. Neo-Confucianism

  1. Background: idealization of past and urge for reform in present

  2. Cosmology and metaphysics: Diagram of the Supreme

Ultimate; the five elements; *li* (principle, or reason) and *ch'i* (material force, matter, or ether) ; influences of Taoism and Buddhism

3. Synthesis of Chu Hsi (1130–1200) : rationalism, reason (or principle, *li*) in all things; in human beings, *li,* as human nature, sometimes distorted by *ch'i,* but correction possible through sincerity *(ch'eng)* and reverence *(ching)* ; sincerity of ruler as basis of political and social order; Chu Hsi as historian

4. Chu Hsi's interpretation of the Classics; the *Four Books;* later acceptance of Chu Hsi's interpretations as orthodox

Reading Assignments
Fitzgerald, *China,* 377–421; 439–54.
Goodrich, *Short History,* 143–63.
Latourette, *The Chinese,* 175–204.
Reischauer and Fairbank, *The Great Tradition,* 193–242.
Sources of Chinese Tradition, 438–91; I, 383–436 (problem of reform) .
510–57; I, 455–502 (Neo-Confucianism) .

Additional Readings
Gernet, Jacques. *Daily Life in China on the Eve of the Mongol Invasion, 1250–1276.* Translated by H. M. Wright. New York: Macmillan, 1962. Paperback, 1969. Absorbing portrait of many facets of life in the Southern Sung capital of Hangchow.
Graham, A. C. *Two Chinese Philosophers: Ch'eng Ming-tao and Ch'eng Yi-ch'uan.* London: Lund Humphries, 1958. A study of the ideas of two of the founders of Neo-Confucianism through a meticulous analysis of their usage of such key terms as *li* (principle) , *ch'i* (ether) , etc. Useful for an understanding of these concepts.
Liu, James T. C., and Peter J. Golas (eds.) . *Change in Sung China: Innovation or Renovation?* Lexington, Mass.: D. C. Heath, 1969. A volume in the Problems in Asian Civilizations series. Selections by leading authorities on change and continuity in economic, political, and intellectual spheres in Sung times, as well as on the more general problem of the periodization of Chinese history.
Liu, James T. C. *Ou-yang Hsiu, An Eleventh-Century Neo-Confucianist.* Stanford: Stanford University Press, 1967. A survey of the political career and the ideas of this important Sung scholar-official.
Liu, James T. C. *Reform in Sung China, Wang An-shih and his*

New Policies. Cambridge: Harvard University Press, 1959. A short interpretive study of the background, implementation, and consequences of Wang's reforms.

Meskill, John (ed.), *Wang An-shih: Practical Reformer?* Boston: D. C. Heath, 1963. A volume in the Problems in Asian Civilizations series. Changing interpretations of Wang and his reforms, with an introductory essay by the editor and an annotated bibliography.

Needham, Joseph. *Science and Civilization in China.* Volumes 1–4. Cambridge: Cambridge University Press, 1954–71. When this projected seven volume work is completed, it will be the most comprehensive treatment of Chinese science in any language. The volumes published to date contain a wealth of information, clearly presented, well organized, and abundantly illustrated. Volume 1 is an excellent survey of the history of Chinese science.

Discussion Questions

1. Neo-Confucianism as an answer to Buddhism; the Confucianism of the Neo-Confucianists; the influence of Buddhist concepts on the system of Chu Hsi.
2. What problems are dealt with by Chu Hsi that were not emphasized by Confucians of the Classical period? of the Han period (Tung Chung-shu)?
3. In what ways did the examination system fail to live up to the ideal method for selecting government officials advocated by the great Confucian thinkers of Chou times? What objections to the examination system did Confucians of Sung times raise?
4. Wang An-shih, his character and policies: his arguments justifying his policies; groups opposed to Wang; arguments of Wang's opponents against his policies. Were Wang An-shih's conservative opponents against reform per se? If not, why did they oppose Wang and his reforms? Assessment of Wang An-shih: practical reformer or headstrong idealist?
5. The rising merchant class: its attitude toward the imperial government; toward the scholar-official class; toward the examination system.
6. The problem of periodization of Chinese history: "unchanging China" or "change within tradition"; applicability of the concept "Early Modern" to late T'ang and Sung China; traditional theory of dynastic cycle; theory of Oriental Despotism ("hydraulic society").
7. Contribution of Chinese inventions to European civilization.

XIII. NON-CHINESE DYNASTIES
  A. Foreign dynasties in north China during Sung period
    1. Liao dynasty (907–1124) ; Mongolic Khitan (Ch'i-tan)
    2. Hsi Hsia dynasty (1038–1227) ; Tibetan Tangut
    3. Chin dynasty (1115–1234) ; Tungusic Jürched (Ju-chen)
  B. Yuan (Mongol) dynasty (1270–1368)
    1. Chinggis Khan (ca. 1167–1227)
      a. Unification of Mongol tribes
      b. Military organization
      c. Campaigns against Liao, Hsi Hsia, and Chin
    2. Mongol conquest of north China (ca. 1206–34)
    3. Conquests in Central and Western Asia
    4. Invasion of south China and end of Sung dynasty (ca. 1251–79)
    5. Khubilai Khan (1215–94; r. 1271–94) as emperor of China
    6. Invasions of Japan (1274 and 1281)
    7. China's place in Mongol Empire
    8. Europeans in Mongol capitals and in Yuan China; Marco Polo
    9. Chinese culture during Yuan dynasty
      a. Painting
      b. Literature
        1) Popular drama (Chinese opera)
        2) Popular novels in colloquial language: *All Men Are Brothers* (*Shui Hu Chuan*) ; *Romance of the Three Kingdoms* (*San Kuo Yen-yi*)
  C. Patterns and problems of barbarian rule
    1. Dual administration: use of Chinese political institutions; non-Chinese in key posts; use of Chinese literati in central and local government; use of language of rulers for affairs of ruling family and Chinese language for affairs of the empire; the Mongol system of categorizing peoples according to reliability (Mongols, Westerners, Northern Chinese, Southern Chinese)
    2. Concessions to and restrictions on Chinese people and Chinese customs
    3. Assimilation of nomadic peoples to sedentary civilization and Chinese culture
    4. Nomadic and tribal values vs. centralized administra-

tion; lack of internal cohesion of ruling non-Chinese peoples
  D. Traditional Chinese policies vs. barbarian peoples
    1. Prevention of tribal confederations
    2. Using barbarians to control barbarians
    3. Absorption into Chinese institutions
       a. Granting of titles, rights, spheres of authority
       b. Marriage alliances
    4. Trade; tribute payments to powerful barbarians

Reading Assignments
Fitzgerald, *China*, 422–38.
Goodrich, *Short History*, 164–88.
Latourette, *The Chinese*, 208–22.
Reischauer and Fairbank, *The Great Tradition*, 243–89.

Additional Readings
Lattimore, Owen. *Inner Asian Frontiers of China*. Second edition. New York: American Geographical Society, 1951. Beacon paperback, 1962. An interpretation of Chinese history that stresses the role played by non-Chinese nomads of the frontiers.
Martin, Desmond. *The Rise of Chingis Khan and His Conquest of North China*. Baltimore: Johns Hopkins Press, 1950. An analysis of the first steps of the Mongol conquest. Especially good on military organization and tactics.
There are many inexpensive editions of Marco Polo's *Travels*. For more specialized study, A. C. Moule, *Quinsai, with other Notes on Marco Polo*. Cambridge: Cambridge University Press, 1957, and A. C. Moule and Paul Pelliot, *Marco Polo: The Description of the World*. London: Routledge, 1938, can be consulted. Interesting use of Marco Polo's writings is made by Etienne Balazs in "Marco Polo in the Capital of China," in Etienne Balazs, *Chinese Civilization and Bureaucracy*, 79–100.

Discussion Questions
1. Discuss the statement "China has always absorbed its conquerors."
2. Compare and contrast pre-T'ang and post-T'ang barbarian states in north China.
3. The impact of barbarian invasions on Chinese civilization: institutions introduced by conquest dynasties; contributions of barbarians to Chinese culture.

4. To what extent did "barbarian rule" of China differ from Chinese rule? In what ways did barbarian rule affect Chinese society?
5. The foreign policy of imperial China: theoretical foundations; the imperial state system; aims and means employed in Chinese foreign policy; critical evaluation of success of means in achieving ends.
6. Problems faced by non-Chinese rulers in ruling China: sinification of non-Chinese ruling peoples; forces tending to encourage sinification; forces tending to impede sinification.

XIV. MING DYNASTY, THE RESTITUTION OF
CHINESE RULE, 1368–1644
Capitals: Nanking and Peking
A. Founding of Ming dynasty
   1. Weaknesses of Yuan
      a. Economic dislocation in south China due to drought, flood, and famine
      b. Rivalries and factional struggles at Yuan court
      c. Chinese dissatisfaction with foreign rule
   2. Chu Yuan-chang (1328–98) as rebel leader
      a. Peasant background and early life as mendicant Buddhist monk
      b. Bandit and rebel leader
      c. Contest with rival rebel leaders for control of Yangtze valley (1362–66)
      d. March north and expulsion of Yuan dynasty
   3. Chu Yuan-chang as emperor: reign of Hung-wu (r. 1368–98)
      a. Establishment of capital at Nanking
      b. Hung-wu's hypersensitivity to personal criticism
      c. Hung-wu's energy and assiduousness as emperor; policy of divide and rule
      d. Abolition of post of prime minister (1380)
      e. Precautions against eunuch power
   4. Reign of Yung-lo (r. 1403–24)
      a. Civil war and usurpation of throne from nephew (1399–1402)
      b. Establishment of new capital at Peking (1421)
      c. Cheng-ho's maritime expeditions to southeast Asia (seven voyages between 1405 and 1433)
B. Later developments: chronic problems and attempted solutions
   1. Military
      a. The Mongol problem
      b. Border defense: garrisons of hereditary armies; professional, self-supporting soldiers (military farmlands)
      c. Japanese pirates
      d. Japanese invasion of Korea (1592–98)
   2. Political
      a. Heavy responsibilities of emperor and growth of

informal cabinet *(nei-ko)* to fill gap after abolition of prime ministership
   b. Imperial power vs. bureaucratic restraints
   c. Reemergence of eunuch power
   d. Standardization of civil service examinations: "eight-legged" essays; Chu Hsi orthodoxy in interpretation of Classics
   e. Bureaucratized education; official schools and private academies
  3. Economic
   a. Proliferation of taxes in early Ming
   b. Tax experiments on local level and trend toward simplification of taxes and tax collection in later Ming (Single Whip Tax, late sixteenth century); payment in silver money
 C. Neo-Confucianism in Ming
  1. Background of the School of Mind; Lu Chiu-yuan (1139–92)
  2. Wang Yang-ming (1472–1529)
   a. His career as a high official
   b. His thought: innate knowledge—moral (and supramoral?) intuition; identity of principle *(li)* and mind; unity of knowledge and action; *jen* as unifying cosmic force; Buddhist influences
   c. Influence of Wang Yang-ming's thought
    1) Political reform movements
    2) Amoral nonconformists
  3. The Eastern Forest Academy *(Tung-lin yuan)* of late Ming
   a. Criticisms of contemporary philosophical trends
   b. Attack on eunuchs and end of academy (1624-26)
 D. Ming literature
  1. Novels: *Monkey (Hsi Yu Chi)* ; *Golden Lotus (Chin P'ing Mei)*
  2. Collections of colloquial short stories

Reading Assignments
Fitzgerald, *China,* 457–72.
Goodrich, *Short History,* 189–213.
Latourette, *The Chinese,* 225–43.
Reischauer and Fairbank, *The Great Tradition,* 290–344.
Sources of Chinese Tradition, 558–81; I, 503–26.

Additional Readings

Gallagher, Louis J. (tr.). *China in the 16th Century: The Journals of Matthew Ricci, 1583–1610*. New York: Random House, 1953. Perceptive comments on Chinese government and society by the alert Jesuit missionary.

Hucker, Charles O. *The Traditional Chinese State in Ming Times (1368–1644)*. Tucson: University of Arizona Press, 1961. A short, general survey of the organization and operations of the government and its relations with society as a whole.

Hucker, Charles O. *The Censorial System of Ming China*. Stanford: Stanford University Press, 1966. The best work on the censorate for any period of Chinese history. Descriptions of the organization and procedures of the various censorial organs, with case studies of their effectiveness.

Mote, Frederick W. *The Poet Kao Ch'i (1336–1374)*. Princeton: Princeton University Press, 1962. Chapter One gives a good account of the rebellions at the end of the Yuan, and of Chu Yuan-chang's triumph over his rivals for the Mandate of Heaven. The remainder of the book centers on the difficulties of one scholar-official, Kao Ch'i, during these years of political instability.

Discussion Questions

1. The censorate as a Confucian institution; as a Legalist institution.

2. The role of education in traditional Chinese society; the scope, purpose, and social effects of education; its limitations; its contribution to social stability.

3. The individual, society, and the state in traditional China.

4. The Wittfogel thesis of Oriental Despotism. What aspects of traditional China does it help to explain? What aspects does it tend to overlook? *

5. The role of eunuchs in the Chinese central government; reasons for their existence; advantages and disadvantages to emperors of relying on eunuchs; reasons for hostility of Confucian scholar-officials toward eunuchs.

6. The Wang Yang-ming school as a political liberalizing force in Ming China; as a restatement of Confucian orthodoxy; as a synthesis of Confucianism with Buddhism and Taoism.

* Karl A. Wittfogel's controversial thesis of "hydraulic societies," of which China is seen as one example, is found in his *Oriental Despotism: A Comparative Study of Total Power*. New Haven: Yale University Press, 1957. Paperback, 1963.

XV. CH'ING DYNASTY, CHINA UNDER MANCHU RULE, 1644–1911, FOUNDATION AND CONSOLIDATION OF CH'ING (to ca. 1800)

Capital: Peking

A. Rebellions at end of Ming
   1. Li Tzu-ch'eng
   2. Chang Hsien-chung
B. Rise of Manchus in north
   1. Origins of Manchu people
   2. Nurhachi (1559–1626) : unification of Jürched tribes; expansion into agricultural areas; titles granted Nurhachi by Ming court; Banner military organization of Manchu tribes; adaptation of Chinese system of administration
   3. Abahai (1592–1643) : consolidation of personal authority of Manchu ruler over tribes; employment of Chinese bureaucrats; establishment of Chinese central government institutions (1631) ; formal proclamation of Ch'ing dynasty (Mukden, 1636) ; subjugation of Korea; raids into north China
C. Manchu conquest of China
   1. Capture of Peking by Li Tzu-ch'eng (1644)
   2. Suppression of Li Tzu-ch'eng by Manchu forces (1644–45)
   3. Manchu control of north China; establishment of Ch'ing capital in Peking (1644)
   4. Ming courts in south China; satrapies in south China
   5. Subjugation of south China and conquest of Taiwan (1673–83)
D. Expansion in Central Asia
   1. Subjugation of Mongols (late seventeenth century)
   2. Subjugation of Tibet (first half of eighteenth century)
   3. Territorial extent of China at height of Ch'ing power
E. Manchu monarchs as Confucian emperors
   1. K'ang-hsi (r. 1661–1722) and the consolidation of Manchu rule; winning the support of the Chinese literati
   2. Ch'ien-lung (r. 1736–95) as Confucian monarch
F. Instruments of Manchu rule
   1. Military: Banner organization; Green Standard Forces
   2. Political: use of Ming institutions; Grand Secretariat and Grand Council (after 1729) ; preponderance of Manchus in key posts in central government; governors

48

and governors-general (viceroys) ; system of checks; rule of avoidance
3. Social: examination system; social mobility and social stability; landholding and examination system; gentry class—definition and functions
4. Intellectual: imperial patronage of classical scholarship; the *Imperial Library* and the Literary Inquisition; continuance of official Chu Hsi orthodoxy; effects of "examination life" on gentry class
5. Reasons for Manchu success in ruling China
G. Chinese thought and culture in early Ch'ing
   1. Reaction to fall of Ming; rejection of intellectual systems of Chu Hsi and Wang Yang-ming
      a. Huang Tsung-hsi (1610–95) : critique of despotism; selflessness of true Prince; need for good men and good laws
      b. Ku Yen-wu (1613–82) : practical learning; empirical method and historical research
      c. Wang Fu-chih (1619–92) : preservation of Chinese race and culture
   2. Search for authentic foundations: textual and historical scholarship; School of Han Learning
   3. Literature
      a. Poetry and theories of poetry
      b. Novels
         1) Social satire: *The Scholars* (*Ju-lin wai-shih*) ; *Flowers in the Mirror* (*Ching-hua-yüan*)
         2) Novel of manners: *Dream of the Red Chamber* (*Hung-lou meng*)
H. Population explosion (ca. 300,000,000 by 1800)
   1. Interacting causes and effects: long period of peace; introduction and spread of new crops from abroad (maize, sweet potato, peanuts, tobacco) ; growth of commerce; increasing pressure on land
   2. Continuing growth of population in nineteenth and twentieth centuries
I. White Lotus Rebellion (1796–1804)
   1. Origins: peasant discontent; tension between religious secret societies and government; anti-Manchu feeling
   2. Decline of Banner forces shown by their ineffectiveness against rebels

Reading Assignments
Fitzgerald, *China,* 541–53.
Goodrich, *Short History,* 214–31.
Latourette, *The Chinese,* 247–68; 450–76.
Reischauer and Fairbank, *The Great Tradition,* 345–93.
Sources of Chinese Tradition, 582–612; I, 527–57.

Additional Readings
Bodde, Derk, and Clarence Morris. *Law in Imperial China: Ex-emplified by 190 Ch'ing Dynasty Cases.* Cambridge: Harvard University Press, 1967. A cooperative effort by a leading sinologist and an expert on Western law, which combines general analysis of the legal system with summaries of illustrative cases.
Ch'ü, T'ung-tsu. *Local Government in China under the Ch'ing.* Cambridge: Harvard University Press, 1962. Stanford paperback, 1969. An analysis of the organization and operations of the lowest level of government in traditional China. Chapter 1, "Chou and Hsien Government," and Chapter 10, "The Gentry and Local Administration," give an excellent description of the structure of local government and of the relationship between state and society on the local level.
Ho, Ping-ti. *The Ladder of Success in Imperial China.* New York: Columbia University Press, 1962. Science Editions paperback, 1964. An outstanding study of social mobility during the Ming and Ch'ing.
Ho, Ping-ti. *Studies on the Population of China, 1368–1953.* Cambridge: Harvard University Press, 1959. A thorough study of population trends, more broad in coverage than the title suggests. A wealth of information on the economy of Ming and early Ch'ing can be found on 169–226.
Hsia, C. T. *The Classic Chinese Novel: A Critical Introduction.* New York: Columbia University Press, 1968. Paperback, 1972. Excellent discussions of the six major pre-modern Chinese novels, giving historical and biographical background as well as literary interpretations.
Hummel, Arthur W. (ed.). *Eminent Chinese of the Ch'ing Period.* Two volumes. Washington: U. S. Government Printing Office, 1943. This biographical dictionary is a standard reference work. The biographies of Nurhachi (I, 594–99), Abahai (I, 1–3), Dorgon (I, 215–19), K'ang-hsi (I, 327–31), and Ch'ien-lung (I, 369–73) are especially informative. For the Manchu conquest, see

also the biographies of Li Tzu-ch'eng (I, 491–93) and Wu San-
kuei (II, 877–80).

Kahn, Harold. *Monarchy in the Emperor's Eyes: Image and Reality in the Ch'ien-lung Reign.* Cambridge: Harvard University Press, 1971. A biographical study of the great eighteenth-century monarch, focusing on the emperor's changing image of himself and his imperial roles.

Menzel, Johanna M. (ed.). *The Chinese Civil Service: Career Open to Talent?* Boston: D. C. Heath, 1963. A volume in the Problems in Asian Civilizations series. Varying interpretations of the examination system, with emphasis on the extent and methods of social mobility through the examinations. Introduction by the editor, and a good, annotated bibliography.

Ts'ao, Hsüeh-ch'in. *Dream of the Red Chamber.* Translated by Chi-chen Wang. New York: Twayne, 1958. Anchor paperback, 1958. China's greatest novel gives a vivid picture of life in an aristocratic household in late traditional China.

Discussion Questions

1. Strengths and weaknesses of the traditional Chinese state. Reasons for its lasting power.
2. The critiques of the imperial system of Huang Tsung-hsi, Wang Fu-chih, and Ku Yen-wu: their extent and limits.
3. Europeans in China before 1800: their problems in dealing with the Chinese government; their contributions to Chinese life.
4. K'ang-hsi and Ch'ien-lung as Confucian monarchs; as foreign rulers.
5. Reasons for the success of the Manchus in ruling China.
6. The civil service examination system and the imperial state. The problem of the proper criteria of "merit": Confucian virtue? knowledge of the Confucian Classics? literary skill? bureaucratic ability? What could the examination system measure? What did the imperial state need?
7. Definitions of the gentry elite: degree holders; landowners.

Modern China

BOOKS FOR ASSIGNED READINGS

Books on Modern China
Fairbank, John King. *The United States and China.* Third edition. Cambridge: Harvard University Press, 1971. Paperback, 1971. An interpretative survey of traditional Chinese society and modern Chinese history by a leading authority. Lucid presentation of major issues; somewhat deficient in factual detail.
Fairbank, John K., Edwin O. Reischauer, and Albert M. Craig. *East Asia: The Modern Transformation.* Boston: Houghton Mifflin, 1965. The companion volume to *East Asia: The Great Tradition,* sophisticated in analysis and filled with fascinating details. Somewhat longer than the other books listed here, and hence not recommended for short survey courses.
Harrison, John A. *China since 1800.* New York: Harcourt, Brace and World, Harbinger paperback, 1967. A good short survey, with brief excerpts from original sources to illustrate the general analysis.
Hsü, Immanuel C. Y. *The Rise of Modern China.* New York: Oxford University Press, 1970. The fullest (over 800 pp.) single-volume textbook treatment. Well-balanced coverage of political, economic, and intellectual history.
McAleavy, Henry. *The Modern History of China.* New York: Praeger, 1967. Paperback, 1967. An objective narrative centering on political history, written in a highly readable style.
Michael, Franz H., and George E. Taylor. *The Far East in the Modern World.* Revised edition. New York: Holt, Rinehart, and Winston, 1964. A smoothly written interpretation of modern Chinese history that emphasizes the role of military power, but does not neglect intellectual currents.

Source Readings
de Bary, Wm. T., Wing-tsit Chan, and Burton Watson (eds.). *Sources of Chinese Tradition.*
Teng, Ssu-yü, and John K. Fairbank (eds.). *China's Response to the West: A Documentary Survey, 1839–1923.* Cambridge: Harvard University Press, 1954. Atheneum paperback, 1966. Much of the material in this excellent collection is duplicated in *Sources of Chinese Tradition,* but this book is useful for its more extensive coverage of a shorter period, and for the valuable introductory comments before each selection.

Supplementary List of Texts and Interpretative Works
Clubb, O. Edmund. *Twentieth Century China.* Second edition. New York: Columbia University Press, 1972. Paperback, 1972. A political history, written in a lively, occasionally polemical style.
Clyde, Paul H., and Burton F. Beers. *The Far East: A History of the Western Impact and the Eastern Response, 1830–1970.* Fifth edition. Englewood Cliffs, N.J.: Prentice-Hall, 1971. Widely used in courses that concentrate on international relations and American Far Eastern policy.
Fitzgerald, C. P. *Birth of Communist China.* New York: Praeger, 1966. Penguin paperback, 1966. (Originally published as *Revolution in China* in 1952.) A stimulating and controversial interpretation of the revolutionary process in modern China, which stresses continuities with the past.

I. EARLY WESTERN CONTACTS WITH CHINA
  A. Missionaries
    1. Roman Catholics and the strategy of accommodation: Matteo Ricci (1552–1610; in Peking 1600–10) and his successors; scientific and scholarly achievements; converts among scholar-officials, but general indifference; Rites Controversy, the problem of compatibility of Confucianism and Catholicism—a religious issue for missionaries, a social and political issue for Chinese government; proscription of Christianity (1724)
    2. Protestants at Hong Kong and Macao in early nineteenth century; missions, schools, journals, hospitals
  B. Sino-Russian relations
    1. Russian expansion into Siberia and trade with China
    2. Border and trade treaties: Nerchinsk (1689), Kiakhta (1727)
    3. Russian ecclesiastical mission and language school in Peking
  C. European merchants
    1. Portuguese, Dutch, and British traders in sixteenth and seventeenth centuries
    2. Foreign trade confined to Canton (1759)
  D. The Canton system
    1. Chinese view of merchants and trade
    2. Chinese view of international relations
    3. East India Company: its monopoly on British trade in Asia; its relations with British government; other trading companies
    4. The system in Canton
      a. Monopoly of Cohong merchants
      b. The Hoppo, the link between merchants and government
      c. Factories and compradors
      d. Trading season
    5. Items of trade: silk and cotton goods; luxury goods; tea; favorable balance of trade for China
    6. Complaints of foreign traders in Canton: numerous and unpredictable petty fees and charges; limitation of trade to Canton and other restrictions on trade by Chinese govern-

ment; Chinese legal practices; aloofness of Chinese officials
7. Attempts by Great Britain to establish diplomatic relations with China
   a. Macartney mission (1793)
   b. Amherst mission (1816)
   c. The kowtow issue

Reading Assignments
Fairbank, Reischauer, and Craig, *The Modern Transformation,* 21–30; 35–79.
Harrison, *China since 1800,* 3–13.
Hsü, *Modern China,* 55–120; 122–212.
McAleavy, *Modern History of China,* 1–35.
Michael and Taylor, *Far East in the Modern World,* 53–56; 119–27.

Additional Readings
Hudson, G. F. *Europe and China.* London: Arnold and Co., 1931. Beacon paperback, 1961. A survey of contacts between China and Europe from early times to the twentieth century.
Hsü, Immanuel C. Y. *China's Entrance into the Family of Nations: The Diplomatic Phase, 1856–1880.* Cambridge: Harvard University Press, 1960. A concise description of the traditional Chinese attitude toward foreign relations is given on 3–18.
Latourette, Kenneth Scott. *A History of Christian Missions in China.* New York: Macmillan, 1929. A standard work by the leading authority. A good survey of Roman Catholic efforts in China from the sixteenth to the eighteenth century can be found on 78–155.
Rowbotham, A. H. *Missionary and Mandarin: The Jesuits at the Court of Peking.* Berkeley: University of California Press, 1942. The problems and accomplishments of the Jesuits in China.

Discussion Questions
1. Compare and contrast European and Chinese attitudes toward commerce in the early nineteenth century.
2. The traditional Chinese view of China and the world. European views of China in the eighteenth century; the nineteenth century; the twentieth century.
3. To what extent was traditional Chinese isolationism based on nationalistic sentiment (nationalism)?

II. EXTERNAL PRESSURES—BREAKDOWN OF THE CANTON SYSTEM AND IMPOSITION OF THE TREATY SYSTEM

A. Deterioration of Canton system
  1. Expansion of trade outside of officially authorized channels: "country trade"; role of American traders; private traders and smugglers
  2. Growth of opium traffic and shift in balance of trade; alarm of Chinese government over detrimental effects of opium smoking and outflow of silver
  3. Abolition of East India Company monopoly on trade with China (1834); ideology of free trade and free traders' political influence in Britain; implications for Canton system
B. Responses to currents of change
  1. Failure of Lord Napier's attempt to establish diplomatic ties on basis of equality (1834); clashes between English and Chinese forces; period of quiescence after Napier's death
  2. Peking's solution to opium problem
    a. Debate on opium trade
      1) Arguments in favor of legalization
      2) Arguments in favor of suppression
    b. Decision to suppress opium trade
C. Showdown at Canton
  1. Chief protagonists and their missions
    a. Sir Charles Elliot (1801–75): background, career, and character; mission as Superintendent of British Trade —expansion of trade in China, to be accomplished through establishment of official ties
    b. Lin Tse-hsü (1785–1850): background, career, and character; mission and authority as Special Commissioner in Canton—to abolish opium trade and retain Canton system; Lin's letter to Queen Victoria as a statement of Chinese view
  2. Issues
    a. Broader problems—the conflict of two cultures: Chinese and Western concepts of interstate relations; Chinese and Western concepts of justice; Chinese and Western ideas about trade; manifestations of these conflicting concepts at Canton
    b. Immediate causes of war: Lin Tse-hsü's confiscation

and destruction of foreign merchants' opium, and demand that merchants guarantee cessation of opium trade; accidental killing of a Chinese by British sailors and Elliot's refusal to permit case to be handled according to Chinese legal procedures

   3. Opium War (1839–42)

     a. Sporadic and localized hostilities

     b. Chinese defeats, reversal in policy, and dismissal of Lin Tse-hsü

     c. Difficulties encountered in peace negotiations

     d. Demonstration of Western power and Chinese weakness

D. Major provisions of treaty settlement

   1. Bilateral treaties of Nanking and The Bogue (with Great Britain, 1842 and 1843), Wang-hsia (with United States, 1844), and Whampoa (with France, 1844)

   2. Provisions

     a. Indemnities

     b. Opening of five ports to trade (Canton, Amoy, Foochow, Ningpo, Shanghai)

     c. Cession of Hong Kong to Great Britain

     d. Fixed, regular, low tariff rate established (loss of tariff autonomy)

     e. Right of extraterritoriality

     f. Most-favored nation clause

   3. Chinese understanding of extraterritoriality and most-favored nation clauses

E. Reactions to first treaty settlement

   1. Chinese

     a. Lin Tse-hsü's reflections in exile

     b. Wei Yuan (1794–1856) and study of the West

     c. Noncompliance with provisions of treaties

   2. Western

     a. Merchants' disappointment with small volume of trade

     b. Dissatisfaction with Chinese response to treaty obligations

     c. Demands for opening of more ports, opening of interior, and diplomatic representation in Peking

     d. Pressures for war

F. Extension of treaty system

   1. Arrow War (1856–60)

     a. The Arrow Incident, the *casus belli*

  b. Capture of Peking, burning of Summer Palace, and flight of emperor

 2. Second treaty settlement

  a. Treaties of Tientsin (1858) and Peking (1860)

  b. Major provisions

   1) Indemnities

   2) Opening of additional coastal ports and Yangtze River

   3) Diplomatic equality and resident ministers in Peking

   4) Legalization of opium trade

   5) Interior opened to propagation of Christianity

 3. Treaties with Russia (1858 and 1860)

  a. Cession of north bank of Amur River and Maritime Province to Russia

  b. Attempt by China to use Russia against other Western Powers

 4. Ramifications of treaty system in late nineteenth and twentieth centuries

  a. Growth of treaty ports: enclaves of Western world in China; means of contact with Western technology, business practices, and ideas; schools of experience for Chinese businessmen and manufacturers; havens for Chinese reformers and revolutionaries; Western experts on China—"Old China Hands" and sinologists

  b. Spread of activities of Christian missionaries

   1) Missionary schools and non-Confucian education

   2) Orphanages and other philanthropic activities

  c. Growth of anti-foreignism in China

   1) Resentment at "unequal treaties"

   2) Hostility toward missionaries; anti-Christianity and anti-foreignism

   3) Anti-foreignism and origins of Chinese nationalism

Reading Assignments

Fairbank, *U.S. and China,* 122–53.

Fairbank, Reischauer, and Craig, *The Modern Transformation,* 80–155; 166–73.

Harrison, *China since 1800,* 14–30.

Hsü, *Modern China,* 214–68.

McAleavy, *Modern History of China,* 36–55.

Michael and Taylor, *Far East in the Modern World,* 127–41.

Sources of Chinese Tradition, 663–79; II, 1–17.

Additional Readings

Banno, Masataka. *China and the West, 1858–1861: The Origins of the Tsungli Yamen.* Cambridge: Harvard University Press, 1964. A careful study of the issue of diplomatic representation in Peking, and its resolution.

Chang, Hsin-pao. *Commissioner Lin and the Opium War.* Cambridge: Harvard University Press, 1964. Norton paperback, 1970. A meticulous study, tracing the drift toward war day by day. Favorable toward Lin Tse-hsü.

Fairbank, John K. *Trade and Diplomacy on the China Coast: The Opening of the Treaty Ports, 1842–1854.* Two volumes in one. Cambridge: Harvard University Press, 1964. Stanford paperback, 1969. The best study of the early years of the treaty ports. The Opium War is viewed from the perspective of modern world history, with much fascinating detail, on 3–151.

Morse, Hosea B. *The International Relations of the Chinese Empire.* Three volumes. London: Longmans, Green, 1910–18. A comprehensive survey of China's relations with the West from 1834 to 1911, which though out of date on some points, still contains much valuable material. Favorable toward the West.

Wakeman, Frederic Jr. *Strangers at the Gate: Social Disorder in South China, 1839–1861.* Berkeley and Los Angeles: University of California Press, 1966. An analysis of the impact of the Opium War on Chinese society in the area surrounding Canton that captures the drama of the social and political tensions raised by the presence of foreign forces on Chinese soil, and the shifting policies of the Chinese government in its attemps to deal with these tensions.

Discussion Questions

1. Lin Tse-hsü's attitude toward opium, and toward his assignment. Was Lin a representative Chinese official? After his arrival in Canton, to what extent did Lin become aware of changes in the situation that had taken place and continued to take place? Compare his fate with that of Yoshida Shoin.
2. Underlying and immediate causes of the Opium War. What broad cultural conflicts can be seen in the particular disputes between the British and Chinese that eventually led to the Opium War? Might the particular disputes have been settled without resort to force? the broader cultural conflicts?
3. Assess the extent of the impact of the West on China in the years after the Opium War; after the Arrow War.

III. INTERNAL DISORDER—REBELLIONS, 1850–1873
A. Taiping Rebellion (1850–64)
1. Background: deterioration of imperial armies and administration; economic problems of population growth; signs of weakness during White Lotus Rebellion (1796–1804)
2. Hung Hsiu-ch'üan (1813–64), the Taiping leader: Hakka background; failures in civil service examinations; contacts with Protestant Christianity (missionaries and tracts); Hung's visions and his concept of mission; the God Worshipers Society
3. Causes of the rebellion
   a. Conflicts between Hakka minority and other groups
   b. Conflicts between inconoclastic God Worshipers Society and local gentry
   c. Peasant unrest
   d. Dislocation and unemployment of inland transport hands arising from shift of trade from Canton to Shanghai
   e. Anti-Manchu feeling
4. Outbreak and spread of rebellion: proclamation of Heavenly Kingdom of Great Peace (1851); various groups that joined Taipings; establishment of capital in Nanking (1853); areas controlled by Taipings; march northward and return to south
5. Taiping ideology: Biblical elements; anti-Confucian element; anti-Manchu element; traditional folk-religious elements; social reforms; equality of women; land system; Taiping ideas in practice
6. Taiping weaknesses: internal dissension, coups and counter-coups within leadership; lack of outstanding leaders in later years; revulsion of gentry
7. Westerners and the Taiping Rebellion
   a. Opinions of Protestant missionaries
   b. Role of foreign-led armies in suppression of Taiping rebellion
   c. Attitudes of Western governments
8. Suppression of the Rebellion
   a. Tseng Kuo-fan (1811–72), the leader of the imperial forces: background and career; organization of professional, local forces from provincial recruits; means of instilling high morale; reorganization of political

63

authority in provinces to finance new local armies; the *likin* (transit) tax; Tseng's gradual acquisition of political and economic power in Hunan; Tseng's Confucianism; his strategy vs. Taipings
  b. Li Hung-chang (1823–1901) and suppression of Taipings in Anhwei
  c. Recapture of Nanking and death of Hung Hsiu-ch'üan (1864)
  B. Other rebellions
    1. Nien rebellion (1853–68) and Tseng Kuo-fan and Li Hung-chang
    2. Moslem rebellions (1855–73) and Tso Tsung-t'ang
  C. Aftermath of rebellions
    1. Economic and administrative dislocation
    2. Trend toward decentralization of power; role of powerful viceroys; implications for future

Reading Assignments
Fairbank, *U.S. and China,* 154–72.
Fairbank, Reischauer, and Craig, *The Modern Transformation,* 155–66; 173–78.
Harrison, *China since 1800,* 30–44.
Hsü, *Modern China,* 270–311.
McAleavy, *Modern History of China,* 56–100.
Michael and Taylor, *Far East in the Modern World,* 178–94.
Sources of Chinese Tradition, 680–704; II, 18–42.

Additional Readings
Hail, William James. *Tseng Kuo-fan and the Taiping Rebellion.* New Haven: Yale University Press, 1927. Reprinted, New York: Paragon Books, 1964. The standard work on the role of the great viceroy in the suppression of the Taipings.
Hummel, Arthur W. (ed.). *Eminent Chinese of the Ch'ing Period.* See Part One, Section XV. The biographies of Hung Hsiu-ch'üan (I, 361–67), Li Hsiu-ch'eng (I, 459–63), and Yang Hsiu-ch'ing (II, 886–88) provide the basic political history of the rebellion.
Kuhn, Philip A. *Rebellion and Its Enemies in Late Imperial China; Militarization and Social Structure, 1796–1864.* Cambridge: Harvard University Press, 1970. Analysis of the shift of local military power from government to gentry due to the Taiping and other rebellions.

Michael, Franz. *The Taiping Rebellion.* Volume I. Seattle: University of Washington Press, 1966. Paperback, 1972. The most extensive narrative account, with much attention given to military aspects.

Shih, Vincent Y. C. *The Taiping Ideology: Its Sources, Interpretations, and Influences.* Seattle: University of Washington Press, 1967. Paperback, 1972. The most exhaustive account of Taiping ideas, of their Chinese and Western origins, and of the historiography of the Taiping Rebellion.

Discussion Questions
1. Similarities and differences between the Taiping Rebellion and previous peasant rebellions in Chinese history.
2. The Taiping Rebellion as a precursor of important trends in twentieth-century China.
3. Different interpretations of the Taiping Rebellion.
4. What held the Chinese empire together during and after the Taiping Rebellion?
5. Culturalism, nationalism, and Christianity in the Taiping Rebellion.

IV. THE RESPONSE TO CHALLENGE: THE T'UNG-CHIH RESTORATION AND SELF-STRENGTHENING

A. Problems of reconstruction after suppression of rebellions
B. The "Cooperative Policy" of the Powers and temporary suspension of pressures on China
C. Calls for reform: the theory of Self-Strengthening
   1. Using Western technology to preserve the Chinese way of life
   2. Feng Kuei-fen (1809–74) : ships, guns, and the natural sciences
   3. Hsueh Fu-ch'eng (1838–94) : changes in methods
   4. Wang T'ao (1828–97) : the need for institutional change
D. Reform measures: Self-Strengthening in practice
   1. Founding of embryonic foreign office (Tsungli Yamen, 1861)
   2. Arsenals and shipyards (Shanghai; Foochow)
   3. Schools for Western languages and technology
   4. Students sent abroad to study
   5. Diplomatic legations established abroad
   6. Burlingame mission to Europe and America
E. Roles of leading viceroys (Tseng Kuo-fan; Li Hung-chang; Tso Tsung-t'ang) and noncoordinated nature of Self-Strengthening
F. Rise to power of the "Empress Dowager," Tz'u-hsi (1835–1908)
   1. Her political acumen and her willfulness
   2. Her conservative proclivity
G. Renewed foreign pressures, and disintegration of the East Asian state system
   1. End of "Cooperative Policy"
      a. Merchant pressures on British government
      b. Tientsin massacre and its impact on European opinion
   2. Japan in the Ryukyu Islands and Formosa (1873)
   3. Conflict with Great Britain: the Margary Affair and concessions in the Chefoo Agreement (1875–76)
   4. War with France and loss of Annam (1883–85)
   5. Response to the new threat
      a. Programs for modernization of armies
      b. Program to modernize navy
      c. Effects of corruption and regionalism on modernization efforts
   6. Struggle with Japan over Korea (1882–95)

a. Interests of China and Japan in Korea
b. Korea's traditional relationship with China
c. Factions at Korean court and Japanese intervention
d. Sino-Japanese War (1894–95)
    1) Destruction of Chinese navy
    2) Rapid victories of Japanese army
e. Treaty of Shimonoseki, amended after Triple Intervention on China's behalf (Germany, France, Russia) ; the final settlement: independence of Korea; huge indemnity; granting of manufacturing rights to Japan in Chinese treaty ports; cession of Formosa
7. "Carving up the Melon"—intensified contest for concessions, spheres of interest, and spheres of influence

Reading Assignments
Fairbank, *U.S. and China,* 173–77.
Fairbank, Reischauer, and Craig, *The Modern Transformation,* 313–84.
Harrison, *China since 1800,* 46–77.
Hsü, *Modern China,* 317–418.
McAleavy, *Modern History of China,* 101–42.
Michael and Taylor, *Far East in the Modern World,* 148–59.
Sources of Chinese Tradition, 705–21; II, 43–59.

Additional Readings
Biggerstaff, Knight. *The Earliest Modern Government Schools in China.* Ithaca, N.Y.: Cornell University Press, 1961. A study of the founding, organization, and operations of the earliest government schools for Western studies.
Hummel, Arthur W. (ed.). *Eminent Chinese of the Ch'ing Period.* The biographies of Tseng Kuo-fan (II, 751–56) and Li Hung-chang (I, 464–71) contain much useful information about these two leading statesmen, and about the years from the 1860s to the end of the century.
Hsü, Immanuel C. Y. *China's Entrance into the Family of Nations.* See Section I, p. 58. Separate sections describe the establishment of foreign legations in Peking, the introduction of international law to China, and the establishment of permanent Chinese legations abroad.
Spector, Stanley. *Li Hung-chang and the Huai Army: A Study in Nineteenth Century Chinese Regionalism.* Seattle: University of Washington Press, 1964. A description of the full range of Li's activities, and of his relations with the central government.

Teng, Ssu-yü, and John K. Fairbank. *China's Response to the West: A Documentary Survey, 1839–1923.* Cambridge: Harvard University Press, 1954. Atheneum paperback, 1966. Although there is some duplication of the readings in *Sources of Chinese Tradition,* pp. 46–83 of this work contain additional material on the Self-Strengthening Movement, with valuable commentaries.

Wright, Mary C. *The Last Stand of Chinese Conservatism: The T'ung-chih Restoration, 1862–1874.* Stanford: Stanford University Press, 1957. Atheneum paperback, 1966. The standard work on the Restoration. Attempts to show how the Confucian social order inhibited China's response to the Western threat.

Discussion Questions

1. Tseng Kuo-fan as a product of traditional Chinese culture and institutions. The focus of his loyalty: the Ch'ing dynasty or Chinese civilization? Was Tseng a nationalist in any sense of the term?
2. Self-Strengthening: goals and limitations.
3. Regionalism in modern China: did it foster or inhibit change?
4. Did the interests of the Manchu rulers differ in any way from those of the Chinese gentry elite? the Chinese people as a whole? Did these differences affect policy?

V. THE FAILURE OF RADICAL REFORM, 1898

A. Chinese reaction to defeat by Japan and to new demands of Western Powers

B. Radical reformers

1. K'ang Yu-wei (1858–1927) : gentry background and education; K'ang's reinterpretation of the past, as in *A Study of the Classics in the Hsin Period* (1891), and *Confucius as a Reformer* (1897) —Confucius as author of the Classics; his purpose the reform of institutions; K'ang's argument for necessity to reform institutions to preserve China; nationalism in K'ang Yu-wei; Confucianism as a faith; K'ang's vision of the future in *The Grand Unity* (*Ta T'ung Shu*) —ideal of one world; idea of progress in K'ang Yu-wei's writings

2. Liang Ch'i-ch'ao (1873–1929), K'ang's chief lieutenant

3. T'an Ssu-t'ung (1865–98) : thoroughgoing westernization; freedom and equality

C. Political activities of reformers

1. Reform societies; journals; memorial of the examination candidates (1895)

2. The reformers in power, the Hundred Days of Reform (1898)

a. The Kuang-hsü Emperor's support of reform

b. Promulgation of reform edicts: education and the examination system; the army; central government administration; plans for local government

c. Overthrow of reformers: role of Yuan Shih-k'ai (1859–1916) ; restoration of Tz'u-hsi to power and withdrawal of Kuang-hsü

d. Fate of reformers: escape of K'ang Yu-wei and Liang Ch'i-ch'ao to Japan; the six martyrs

e. Reasons for failure of K'ang Yu-wei's attempt at reform

1) Groups hostile to reforms

2) Objections of Confucian conservatives; institutions as ends, not means

D. Persistence of reform ideas

1. Moderate reform, as in the program of Chang Chih-tung (1837–1909) ; Chang's *Exhortation to Study* (1898) : its extraordinary popularity; "Chinese studies as the foundaion; Western studies as the means"; reinvigoration of traditional ethical principles; dangers to social order of

69

individualism, egalitarianism, and democracy; need for military, industrial, and educational modernization
2. Full-scale westernization and translations of Yen Fu (1854–1921) ; Social Darwinism; liberalism; the need to strengthen the country, and incipient nationalism

Reading Assignments
Fairbank, *U.S. and China,* 177–81.
Fairbank, Reischauer, and Craig, *The Modern Transformation,* 384–407; 468–77.
Harrison, *China since 1800,* 78–86.
Hsü, *Modern China,* 423–57.
McAleavy, *Modern History of China,* 143–60.
Michael and Taylor, *Far East in the Modern World,* 194–201.
Sources of Chinese Tradition, 721–59; II, 59–97.

Additional Readings
Cameron, Meribeth E. *The Reform Movement in China, 1898–1912.* Stanford: Stanford University Press, 1931. Reprinted, New York: Octagon Books, 1963. The Hundred Days of Reform are discussed on 23–55.
Hsiao, Kung-ch'üan. "K'ang Yu-wei and Confucianism," *Monumenta Serica,* XVIII (1959), 96–212, and "The Philosophical Thought of K'ang Yu-wei: An Attempt at a New Synthesis," *Monumenta Serica,* XXI (1962), 129–93. "The Case for Constitutional Monarchy: K'ang Yu-wei's Plan for the Democratization of China," *Monumenta Serica,* XXIV (1965), 1–83. The most exhaustive treatments of Kang's thought in English.
Schwartz, Benjamin I. *In Search of Wealth and Power: Yen Fu and the West.* Cambridge: Harvard University Press, 1964. Harper Torchbook, 1969. The views of the West of the translator of Darwin, Huxley, Montesquieu, J. S. Mill, and Herbert Spencer, as seen in his commentaries to translations. A valuable study which throws light on the emergence of nationalism in modern China.
Smith, Arthur H. *Village Life in China.* New York: Fleming H. Revell, 1899. Little Brown paperback, with new Introduction by Myron L. Cohen, 1970. Colorful descriptions of village life in late imperial China by a Protestant missionary with strong biases, whose long residence in rural China made him familiar with the everyday life of the people.

Discussion Questions

1. In 1898, all groups professed the desire to save China. What did "China" mean to the conservatives? to K'ang Yu-wei? What significance do you see in these different conceptions of "China"?
2. What lessons can be drawn from the failure of K'ang Yu-wei's attempt at reform?
3. Obstacles to K'ang's plans. What objections did conservatives make to K'ang's proposals and to his methods? Evaluate the validity of these objections. In what ways were the conservatives' objections to thorough Westernization more perceptive than the views of the radical reformers? Who was more "realistic"?
4. Compare the goals and programs of Chang Chih-tung with those of Feng Kuei-fen and Hsueh Fu-ch'eng. Are there any significant differences? Compare the pace of demand for and implementation of reform in late Ch'ing China and late Tokugawa and Meiji Japan. What could any differences be attributed to?
5. The role of the individual in history: the character, beliefs, and policies of Tz'u-hsi as factors deterring modernization in late nineteenth-century China. If a reform-minded ruler had held power, might the response to the West have been different? Could a reform-minded ruler have come to power?
6. What was Tz'u-hsi defending? the Manchu monarchy? the Chinese empire? the Confucian system? her own position?
7. Evaluate Tz'u-hsi and K'ang Yu-wei as politicians.

VI. DISINTEGRATION OF THE MONARCHY: REACTION AND REFORM, 1898–1911

A. Boxer Rebellion (1898–1901)
   1. Origins of the Boxer movement
      a. Secret societies
      b. Anti-foreign sentiment
      c. Resentment at missionary activities and anti-Christian sentiment
   2. Divergent policies of Ch'ing officials toward Boxers
      a. Encouragement from Manchu and reactionary officials
      b. Suppression by other officials, e.g. Yuan Shih-k'ai
      c. Spread of Boxer movement in areas under authority of pro-Boxer officials
      d. The Boxers in Peking; siege of the legations
      e. Role of Tz'u-hsi in encouraging Boxers; declaration of war on Powers
      f. Conciliatory policy of Viceroys of southern provinces
   3. The foreign expeditionary force
      a. Defeat of Boxers and fall of Peking
      b. Flight of emperor and Tz'u-hsi from capital
   4. Boxer Protocol
      a. Huge indemnities
      b. Punishment of officials judged culpable by Powers
   5. Tensions between Japan and Russia in Manchuria
B. Military reforms and power of Yuan Shih-k'ai
   1. Further modernization of Chinese army
   2. Position of Yuan Shih-k'ai after deaths of Tz'u-hsi and Kuang-hsü Emperor (1908), and Chang Chih-tung (1909)
   3. Forced retirement of Yuan (1909)
C. Educational reforms
   1. Abolition of civil service examination system (1905)
   2. Spread of modern schools and Western studies
   3. Founding of Peking University
D. Political reforms
   1. Activities of Liang Ch'i-ch'ao: journalism; the need to "Renew the People"; Liang's estrangement from K'ang Yu-wei
   2. Constitutional movement: agitation in the provinces; impact of Japanese victory in Russo-Japanese War (1905); promises wrested from Manchu court; formation of first cabinet (1911)
E. Controversy over financing railroad construction

1. Failure of provincial financing schemes
2. Provincial opposition to railroad construction under direction of central government
3. Consortium loan to central government and crisis in Szechwan (Sept. 1911)

Reading Assignments
Fairbank, *U.S. and China*, 181–92.
Fairbank, Reischauer, and Craig, *The Modern Transformation*, 613–31.
Harrison, *China since 1800*, 86–92.
Hsü, *Modern China*, 460–536.
McAleavy, *Modern History of China*, 161–70.
Michael and Taylor, *Far East in the Modern World*, 201–09.

Additional Readings
Levenson, Joseph R. *Liang Ch'i-ch'ao and the Mind of Modern China*. Cambridge: Harvard University Press, 1955. University of California paperback, 1967. An intellectual biography of Liang from his earliest reform period through his conservative reaction against the West in the 1920s.
Powell, Ralph L. *The Rise of Chinese Military Power, 1895–1912*. Princeton: Princeton University Press, 1955. An informative study of the modernization of the Chinese army, and of the rise of Yuan Shih-k'ai.
Tan, Chester C. *The Boxer Catastrophe*. New York: Columbia University Press, 1955. Concentrates on the diplomatic aspects of the Boxer settlement.

Discussion Question
1. What animated the Boxer rebels? Motives of Chinese and Manchu officials who supported the Boxers; of the Empress Dowager; of officials who suppressed the Boxers.
2. Did reforms after the Boxer Rebellion contribute to or deter the the rising tide of revolution?

VII. THE REVOLUTION OF 1911

A. The revolutionary movement
   1. Sun Yat-sen (1866–1925) : family background; Western education; formation of revolutionary organizations; travels in Europe and America; the T'ung Meng Hui; the Three Peoples Principles (nationalism, democracy, people's livelihood) ; the Chinese people as a "heap of loose sand"; single tax and equalization of land; the Three Stages of Revolution and role of revolutionary elite; sources of Sun's ideas
   2. Other revolutionary leaders: Huang Hsing; Sung Chiao-jen
   3. Goals of revolutionaries: defense of Chinese sovereignty; elimination of Manchu rule; replacement of monarchy by republic; economic transformation
   4. Unsuccessful uprisings in south China (1906–11)
B. Revolt in south China
   1. Uprising at Wuhan (Oct. 10, 1911)
   2. Declarations of independence of southern provinces
   3. Response of Manchu court to crisis; recall of Yuan Shih-k'ai on Yuan's terms
C. End of Ch'ing dynasty
   1. Reliance of Manchu court on Yuan Shih-k'ai's armies
   2. Yuan's aims and strategy of delay
   3. Weaknesses of revolutionaries
      a. Divided counsels
      b. Lack of military strength
   4. Return of Sun Yat-sen to China: Sun's agreement with Yuan
   5. Abdication of Manchu emperor
   6. Yuan Shih-k'ai as President of the Republic

Reading Assignments

Fairbank, *U.S. and China,* 192–94.

Fairbank, Reischauer, and Craig, *The Modern Transformation,* 631–42.

Harrison, *China since 1800,* 93–100.

Hsü, *Modern China,* 538–64.

McAleavy, *Modern History of China,* 171–86.

Michael and Taylor, *Far East in the Modern World,* 209–18.

Sources of Chinese Tradition, 760–86; II, 98–124.

Additional Reading

Gasster, Michael. *Chinese Intellectuals and the Revolution of 1911: The Birth of Modern Chinese Radicalism*. Seattle: University of Washington Press, 1969. Excellent analysis of currents of political and social thought among Chinese radicals and revolutionaries in the early twentieth century, focusing on issues more than on individuals.

Sharman, Lyon. *Sun Yat-sen, His Life and Its Meaning: A Critical Biography*. New York: John Day, 1934. Reprinted, Stanford: Stanford University Press, 1968. Paperback, 1968. Still the best biography of Sun available.

Wright, Mary C. (ed.). *China in Revolution: The First Phase, 1900–1913*. New Haven: Yale University Press, 1968. Paperback, 1971. A superbly edited collection of articles on all facets of the revolution: social classes, provincial organizations, political groups, and individual leaders. Stresses extent of change during last years of monarchy. Indispensable.

Discussion Questions

1. The utopian visions of K'ang Yu-wei and Sun Yat-sen; elements in common; differences.
2. Compare Liang Ch'i-ch'ao and Sun Yat-sen: background and education; analysis of China's weakness; proposals to overcome this weakness; visions of the future. How "Westernized" were they?
3. Interpretations of the Revolution of 1911: the first true revolution in Chinese history; a political but not a social revolution. To what extent does the overthrow of the Manchu dynasty deserve to be called a revolution at all?
4. Were the revolutionary movement and the outbreak at Wuhan merely catalysts for more powerful centrifugal forces long latent? Did these centrifugal forces have anything in common?
5. Which was more revolutionary, the abolition of the examination system in 1905 or the overthrow of the Manchu dynasty (and the dynastic system) in 1911?

VIII. FALTERING SEARCH FOR POLITICAL ORDER
AND REJECTION OF THE MONARCHICAL
PRINCIPLE, 1912–1917
  A. Yuan Shih-k'ai vs. Parliament; establishment of primacy
     of the executive
     1. Provisional Constitution
     2. Dispute over constitutional powers of President and
        Prime Minister
     3. Failure of "Second Revolution" (July–August 1913)
        against Yuan Shih-k'ai
     4. Yuan's victory over Parliamentary opposition
        a. Forced dissolution of Kuomintang (1913)
        b. Suspension of Parliament (1914)
  B. Yuan Shih-k'ai's search for foreign support
     1. Concessions and loans; Reorganization Loan (April
        1913)
     2. Recognition of Chinese Republic by Powers (Oct. 1913)
     3. Japan's Twenty-One Demands (Jan. 1915)
        a. Expansion of Japanese influence in China while
           European Powers involved in World War I
        b. Yuan's acceptance of Japanese ultimatum
        c. Indignation of patriotic Chinese
  C. Yuan Shih-k'ai's campaign to become emperor (1914–16)
     1. Limited support for Yuan's plan
     2. Widespread opposition to Monarchical movement: Kuo-
        mintang; Liang Ch'i-ch'ao; parliamentary forces;
        Japan; Yuan's generals
     3. Collapse of movement and death of Yuan Shih-k'ai
        (1916)
  D. Rapid collapse of attempt to restore Manchu monarchy
     (1917)
  E. Fragmentation of authority after death of Yuan Shih-k'ai
     1. Emergence of warlords (tuchün); military power as
        chief source of political influence
     2. Warlord groupings and warlord politics; kaleidoscopic
        governments in Peking (1916–28)

Reading Assignments
Fairbank, *U.S. and China*, 195–201.

Fairbank, Reischauer, and Craig, *The Modern Transformation,* 642–58.
Harrison, *China since 1800,* 100–10.
Hsü, *Modern China,* 564–76.
McAleavy, *Modern History of China,* 187–200.
Michael and Taylor, *Far East in the Modern World,* 218–25.

Additional Readings

Bianco, Lucien. *Origins of the Chinese Revolution, 1915–1949.* Translated by Muriel Bell. Stanford: Stanford University Press, 1971. Superb interpretative survey of modern Chinese history from the intellectual revolution to the Communist victory in the civil war, stressing social forces which brought the Communists to power.

Ch'en, Jerome. *Yuan Shih-k'ai, 1859–1916.* Second edition. Stanford: Stanford University Press, 1972. A political biography of Yuan, which shows some sympathy for Yuan's problems as chief of state in the years after the revolution.

Clubb, O. Edmund. *Twentieth Century China.* Second edition. New York: Columbia University Press. 1972. Paperback, 1972. The political history of the revolution and the years immediately following is described on 36–80.

Sheridan, James E. *Chinese Warlord: The Career of Feng Yü-hsiang.* Stanford: Stanford University Press, 1966. Paperback, 1970. A political biography of one of the most important warlords of north China. Chapter 1, "Emergence of the Warlords," traces the evolution of militarism from the Taiping Rebellion to the mid-1920s.

Discussion Questions

1. The significance of the failure of Yuan Shih-k'ai's attempt to restore monarchy.
2. The political role of military power in modern China, from Tseng Kuo-fan to Mao Tse-tung. The role of military power and military groups in the modernization of China.
3. Did liberal democracy have a chance in China at any time in the twentieth century? If so, when? Why did it fail? Precedents for democracy in the Chinese tradition: in political and social thought; in practice.
4. In what ways were the warlords products of their times? responsible for conditions in China during their times?

77

IX. EMERGENCE OF NEW FORCES: THE NEW CULTURE MOVEMENT

A. Intellectual ferment in Peking: education and Westernization
   1. Ts'ai Yuan-p'ei (1867–1940) as Chancellor of Peking University; academic freedom and Western studies
   2. Ch'en Tu-hsiu (1879–1942) and *New Youth* magazine (*Hsin Ch'ing-nien*) : attack on Confucianism and rejection of the past; key Western values—Science and Democracy; equality for women
   3. Hu Shih (1891–1962) : education, pragmatism, and democracy; adoption of colloquial Chinese as the literary language; Hu's career as educator
B. May Fourth Movement: the birth of nationalism as a social and political force
   1. Popular expectations from Chinese participation in World War I
   2. China at the Versailles Conference; impact in China of decision to transfer German rights in China to Japan; the Shantung Question
   3. Student demonstrations, beginning May 4, 1919 in Peking
   4. Rapid spread of student and merchant strikes and boycotts
   5. Resignation of pro-Japanese cabinet ministers
C. Westernization of Chinese intelligentsia: intellectual life in the 1920s
   1. New Culture Movement: spread of use of colloquial Chinese as written language; proliferation of periodicals
   2. John Dewey and Bertrand Russell in China (1919–20)
   3. Ku Chieh-kang (1893–   ) and the doubting of antiquity;   re-evaluation of China's history and historical heritage
   4. Modern Chinese fiction
      a. Influence of European literature; emphasis on plot, character, realism
      b. Translations from Western literature
      c. Novels and short stories; the social satire of Lu Hsün (1881–1936) ; tension between hope and despair as a common theme
      d. Literary societies and theories of literature; art for art's sake vs. art for the sake of society

5. Controversy over relative merits of Eastern and Western cultures (1922–   )
   a. Liang Ch'i-ch'ao's disillusionment with materialism of West
   b. Liang Shu-ming (1893–   ) : value of Chinese humanism; intuitive knowledge; harmony with the universe
   c. Hu Shih's defense of spiritual values of West
6. Debate on Science and Metaphysics (1923)
   a. Chang Chün-mai (Carsun Chang, 1886–1968) : limited scope of scientific method; science and the material world; metaphysics and world of the human spirit
   b. Faith in science of V. K. Ting and Hu Shih
D. Organizing the new social forces
   1. Labor unions, in treaty ports
   2. YMCA and YWCA
   3. Anarchists
   4. Chinese Communist Party (CCP)
      a. Impact of Russian Revolution on China: Li Ta-chao (1889–1927) and the message of Bolshevism
      b. *New Youth* magazine and introduction of Marxism
      c. Marxist study groups (1919–20)
      d. First Congress of CCP (Shanghai, 1921)
         1) Role of Comintern agents in founding CCP
         2) Ch'en Tu-hsiu as Secretary General
      e. Membership of CCP
         1) Numerically small
         2) Western-oriented intelligentsia

Reading Assignments
Fairbank, *U.S. and China,* 201–07.
Fairbank, Reischauer, and Craig, *The Modern Transformation,* 658–72.
Harrison, *China since 1800,* 110–25.
Hsü, *Modern China,* 581–602.
McAleavy, *Modern History of China,* 201–27.
Michael and Taylor, *Far East in the Modern World,* 225–35.
Sources of Chinese Tradition, 813–57; II, 151–95.

Additional Readings
Chow, Tse-tsung. *The May Fourth Movement: Intellectual Revolution in Modern China.* Cambridge: Harvard University Press,

1960. Stanford paperback, 1967. Covers the whole range of the movement, from student and merchant demonstrations to intellectual debates.

Grieder, Jerome B. *Hu Shih and the Chinese Renaissance: Liberalism in the Chinese Revolution, 1917–1937*. Cambridge: Harvard University Press, 1970. Excellent intellectual biography of the most prominent modern Chinese liberal thinker.

Harrison, James P. *History of the Chinese Communist Party*. New York: Praeger, 1972. Paperback, 1972. The fullest, most up-to-date history of the first fifty years of the CCP.

Hsia, C. T. *A History of Modern Chinese Fiction*. Second edition. New Haven: Yale University Press, 1971. Paperback, 1971. Critical discussions of the major writers and important literary movements and organizations.

Levenson, Joseph R. "The Intellectual Revolution in Modern China," in Albert Feuerwerker (ed.), *Modern China*. Prentice-Hall, Spectrum paperback, 1964, 154–68. A stimulating interpretation of main intellectual currents in China from the Opium War to the Communists. (This book contains a number of excellent articles.)

Meisner, Maurice. *Li Ta-chao and the Origins of Chinese Marxism*. Cambridge: Harvard University Press, 1967. Atheneum paperback, 1970. An intellectual biography of one of the founders of the CCP. A good summary of the introduction of Marxism into China is given on 52–70.

Schwartz, Benjamin I. *Chinese Communism and the Rise of Mao*. Cambridge: Harvard University Press, 1951. Harper Torchbook, 1967. An important work, which though outdated in some respects, is still useful for the early history of the CCP.

Discussion Questions

1. Culturalism and nationalism in modern China. Distinguish between culturalism and nationalism. When does nationalism begin to emerge? When does it become an important social and historical force? When does it become a revolutionary force?
2. The attitude toward science of Chinese intellectuals, from 1919 to the present.
3. Compare arguments of conservatives after 1919 with those of nineteenth-century conservatives.
4. Christianity and the New Culture Movement. The role of Christian missionaries in modern Chinese history.

X. REORGANIZATION OF THE KUOMINTANG AND MILITARY UNIFICATION OF CHINA

A. Sun Yat-sen's misadventures, 1914–22
1. Organization of Kemingtang (Revolutionary Party, 1914) ; secret, conspiratorial party; personal allegiance of members to Sun
2. Sun's involvement in political struggles in Kwangtung, 1917–18
3. Organization of Kuomintang (Nationalist Party, KMT, 1919) ; open political party
4. Sun and warlord politics in Kwangtung, 1921–22

B. Sun Yat-sen's alliance with Soviet Russia
1. Sun's lack of success in obtaining aid from Western Powers
2. Comintern policy and Soviet aims in China: revolution in colonial and semicolonial countries as means to weaken world imperialism
3. Sun-Joffe joint declaration on Sino-Soviet relations (1923)
4. Soviet aid to KMT: weapons; political and military advisers
5. New elements in KMT ideology: nationalism as equality of peoples within China; land to the tillers; nationalization of major industries; use of propaganda appeals to masses

C. Reorganization of KMT
1. Roles of Michael Borodin and other Russian advisers
2. Principle of democratic centralism; intraparty democracy and intraparty discipline; authority of Central Executive Committee of KMT
3. Ratification of reorganization by First National Congress of KMT (Canton, 1924)
4. First United Front with CCP; members of CCP admitted to KMT as individuals; role of Comintern advisers in formation of united front
5. Whampoa Military Academy; training a party army
6. Assertion of KMT power in Canton
7. Sudden death of Sun Yat-sen

D. Chiang Kai-shek's rise to power
1. Strife among successors to Sun Yat-sen; elimination of left-wing and right-wing leaders of KMT (assassination of Liao Chung-k'ai; forced retirement of Hu Han-min)
2. Emergence of new leaders within KMT
   a. Chiang Kai-shek (1887–   ) : gentry background; mil-

itary education; early revolutionary activities; conversion to Christianity; Commandant of Whampoa Military Academy
  b. Wang Ching-wei (1883–1944): character and early revolutionary fame; leader of left wing of KMT
3. Labor movement and May 30 incident (1925)
  a. Revulsion at shooting of demonstrators and upsurge of national feeling
  b. Wave of strikes
  c. Growth of membership of CCP and KMT; strengthening of left wing within KMT
4. Growing influence of CCP members within KMT; Chiang's reaction: coup against Communists and Russian advisers (March 1926); compromise settlement between Chiang and Communists
5. The Northern Expedition and split within KMT
  a. Strengthening of KMT position in Kwangtung and Kwangsi
  b. Sun Yat-sen's ideal of a Northern Expedition to reunify China
  c. First stages of Northern Expedition: campaigns against Yangtze warlords; popular support of KMT armies; absorption of many warlord armies into KMT armies
  d. Transfer of revolutionary government from Canton to Wuhan (1926); domination of government by left wing
  e. Chiang Kai-shek's acquisition of allies on the right; ties with Shanghai bankers and business groups; agreements with warlords
  f. Chiang's suppression of Communists and labor unions in Shanghai and Nanking
  g. Chiang's establishment of rival KMT government (Nanking, April 1927)
  h. Formal expulsion of Chiang from KMT by Wuhan government (April 1927)
  i. Stalin's policy directives to CCP, and split between Wuhan government and Communists (July 1927); Wang Ching-wei's loss of support and retirement
6. Reunification of KMT under leadership of Chiang Kai-shek
E. Culmination of Northern Expedition
1. Political situation in north China in 1926–27; wars between rival warlords

2. Rapid march northward of KMT armies; capture of Peking; submission of northern warlords
3. Proclamation of National Government of China (Nanking, 1928)
4. Clash between KMT armies and Japanese troops at Tsingtao, omen of the future
F. Impact within CCP of split with KMT
   1. Dismissal of Ch'en Tu-hsiu as Secretary General (1927)
   2. Implementation of radical policies
      a. Mao Tse-tung (1893–   ) : peasant background; early education; activities as member of CCP; Mao's "Report on an Investigation of the Hunan Peasant Movement" (1927) —vital role of peasantry in Chinese revolution, and leadership of poor peasantry
      b. Mao Tse-tung and the Autumn Harvest Uprisings (Sept. 1927)
      c. Canton Commune (Dec. 1927)
   3. Rapid decline in CCP membership

Reading Assignments
Fairbank, *U.S. and China,* 207–15.
Fairbank, Reischauer, and Craig, *The Modern Transformation,* 673–91.
Harrison, *China since 1800,* 125–41.
Hsü, *Modern China,* 604–30.
McAleavy, *Modern History of China,* 228–58.
Michael and Taylor, *Far East in the Modern World,* 329–39; 371–89.
Sources of Chinese Tradition, 858–77; II, 196–215.

Additional Readings
Brandt, Conrad. *Stalin's Failure in China, 1924–1927.* Cambridge: Harvard University Press, 1958. Norton Library paperback, 1966. A study of Russian influence on the policies of the CCP during the years of the first KMT-CCP united front.
Liu, F. F. *A Military History of Modern China, 1924–1949.* Princeton: Princeton University Press, 1956. A good survey. An analysis of Chiang Kai-shek's rise to power and the Northern Expedition, 3–59.
Wilbur, C. Martin, "Military Separatism and the Process of Reunification under the Nationalist Regime," in Ping-ti Ho and Tang Tsou (eds.), *China in Crisis.* Vol. I, Part I. Chicago: University of Chicago Press, 1968. Paperback, 1970. Pp. 203–63. Concise survey of the role of the military in Chinese politics, concen-

trating on the Nationalist armies from the Northern Expedition to outbreak of war with Japan. (This book contains many other excellent articles.)

Discussion Questions
1. The development of political parties in modern China. Their relations with the traditional elite, with military forces, and with parliamentary and revolutionary movements.
2. Was Sun Yat-sen's alliance with Soviet Russia a radical shift in his political behavior? Did it involve any inconsistency with his previously proclaimed viewpoints?
3. Was the split that ended the First United Front the result of a struggle between two groups seeking political power, or does it demonstrate some inherent conflict between nationalism and communism?
4. The relationship between anti-imperialism and social revolution in modern China.

XI. THE NATIONAL GOVERNMENT IN POWER, 1928–1937

A. Limited nature of authority of National Government
1. Rivals in provinces; autonomy of warlords; compromise pacts and formal submission of warlords; shifting alignments of warlords
2. Areas under direct administrative control of National Government
   a. Yangtze provinces
   b. Port cities
B. Structure of National Government
1. Theoretical basis of KMT domination of National Government: the period of tutelage and party rule
2. Constitutions: Organic Law (1928) ; Provisional Constitution (1931)
3. Five-Power Government: Executive Yuan; Legislative Yuan; Judicial Yuan; Examination Yuan; Control Yuan (Censorate) ; combination of traditional Chinese and Western institutions
C. Elements supporting National Government
1. Intelligentsia
2. Bureaucracy
3. Financiers and industrialists in treaty ports
4. Landholding classes
D. Basis of personal power of Chiang Kai-shek
1. Chiang's offices in KMT, National Government, and army
2. Groups supporting Chiang
   a. T. V. Soong, H. H. Kung, and financial circles
   b. The "CC Clique" and the KMT apparatus
   c. The Whampoa Clique and the army
E. Accomplishments of National Government
1. Domestic: reorganization of finances (currency reform, 1935) ; modernization of army; communications (railroads, shipping) ; municipal modernization; education; legal reforms (civil and penal codes) ; problems of implementation, exploratory commissions, planning boards, and paper legislation
2. Foreign: recovery of tariff autonomy; progress in drive to end unequal treaties
F. Problems facing National Government
1. Domestic

a. Autonomous warlords; sporadic revolts, compromise settlements, and steady reduction of power of military rivals
b. Dissatisfied intelligentsia
1) The debate on political tutelage: needs of the nation vs. rights of the people
2) Opposition of influential intellectuals; League of Left-Wing Writers
3) The New Life Movement as a response to dissatisfaction among intelligentsia; call for adherence to Confucian virtues; influence of Christianity
c. CCP, 1928–37
1) Moscow-directed party headquarters: leadership drawn from urban intelligentsia; policies concentrated on revolution in cities; repeated failures, and turnovers in leadership
2) Rural-based military organization: Mao Tse-tung, Chu Te, and Red Army; Kiangsi Soviet Government (1931–34); radical land policy of Soviet Government; Chiang Kai-shek's extermination campaigns and CCP tactics of guerilla warfare
3) The Long March and emergence of Mao Tse-tung as undisputed leader of CCP (1934–35)
4) CCP in Yenan
d. Peasantry
1) The land problem: population growth and production increases; increase in tenancy rate
2) Handicraft industries: role in traditional peasant economy; loss of some markets to imported low-priced manufactured goods; new handicrafts and new markets; impact on rural economy
2. Foreign
a. Soviet Russia; clashes with Soviet Army
b. Japan; Manchurian Incident (1931); founding of Manchukuo (1932); absorption of Jehol Province (1933); Japanese pressures on north China

Reading Assignments

Fairbank, *U.S. and China,* 215–39.
Fairbank, Reischauer, and Craig, *The Modern Transformation,* 691–706.
Harrison, *China since 1800,* 143–64.
Hsü, *Modern China,* 633–72.
McAleavy, *Modern History of China,* 259–96.

Michael and Taylor, *Far East in the Modern World,* 389–422.
Sources of Chinese Tradition, 786–812; II, 124–50.

Additional Readings

Ch'ien, Ţuan-sheng. "The Kuomintang: Its Doctrine, Organization, and Leadership," in Albert Feuerwerker (ed.), *Modern China,* 70–88. An unsympathetic analysis of the internal structure of the KMT.

Clubb, O. Edmund. *Twentieth Century China.* A highly critical account of the accomplishments and failures of the National Government is given on 149–217.

Fei, Hsiao-t'ung. *Peasant Life in China.* London: Routledge, 1939. Reprinted, 1962. An outstanding field study of a peasant village, by a leading Chinese anthropologist. Illustrated.

Israel, John. *Student Nationalism in China, 1927–1937.* Stanford: Stanford University Press, 1967. Analyzes student political views and activities, centering on relations with the KMT and CCP.

Sih, Paul K. T. (ed.). *The Strenuous Decade: China's Nation-Building Efforts, 1927–1937.* New York: St. John's University Press, 1970. Collection of articles, favorable to efforts toward political and economic reconstruction of the Nationalist government.

Snow, Edgar. *Red Star over China.* New York: Random House, 1938. Grove paperback, 1968. The classic account of the fortunes of the Communists from 1927 to the Sino-Japanese War. Mao Tse-tung's autobiography, as told to Snow, is a major historical document.

Wright, Mary C. "The Heritage of the Restoration" in *The Last Stand of Chinese Conservatism,* 300–12. An analysis of KMT ideology after 1928, stressing its conservative character.

Discussion Questions

1. Can China under KMT rule be termed a dictatorship?
2. Strengths and weaknesses of the KMT, 1928–37; 1937–49.
3. The growing conservatism of the Kuomintang in the 1930s. In what ways was this typical of any revolutionary group once it attains power? What special factors operated in the case of the KMT?
4. Christianity and Confucianism in the ideology of the KMT in the 1930s.
5. Did the National Government fulfill or abandon the principles of Sun Yat-sen?
6. The relations between the CCP and Moscow, 1921–35. Moscow's role in Mao Tse-tung's rise to power within the CCP.

XII. SINO-JAPANESE WAR AND WORLD WAR II, 1937–1945

A. Formation of Second United Front
  1. CCP policy toward Japanese threat
  2. Protests against National Government's policy of subduing domestic opposition before facing Japanese threat
  3. New Comintern line on United Front (1935)
  4. Kidnaping of Chiang Kai-shek, the Sian Incident (1936)
  5. Second United Front of KMT and CCP; negotiations, concessions on both sides, and temporary accommodation
B. Second Sino-Japanese War
  1. Japanese demands on north China
  2. Outbreak of hostilities (1937)
  3. Rapid Japanese victories; capture of north China; capture of sea coast and port cities
  4. Evacuation of Nationalist capital to Chungking (1938)
  5. Japanese-sponsored puppet government of Wang Ching-wei
  6. Numerical growth and territorial expansion of Red Army
  7. Competition for territory between CCP and National Government
  8. Inflation
  9. The ideological struggle
    a. Mao's program for China, in *On New Democracy* (1940) : the Chinese Revolution and world revolution; modifications in CCP land program; alignment of revolutionary classes
    b. Chiang's program for China, in *China's Destiny* (1943) : significance of abolition of unequal treaties; reconstruction of China under KMT leadership; importance of Chinese values and detrimental effects of exaggerated admiration of the West
  10. Conflicts between Chiang Kai-shek and American advisers
  11. China's role in allied victory in Asia
C. China's gains from World War II
  1. End of extraterritoriality (1943)
  2. Recognition of China as a Great Power
  3. Restitution of Manchuria and Taiwan

Reading Assignments
Fairbank, *U.S. and China,* 240–58.
Fairbank, Reischauer, and Craig, *The Modern Transformation,* 706–17.
Harrison, *China since 1800,* 165–85.
Hsü, *Modern China,* 676–710.
McAleavy, *Modern History of China,* 297–321.
Michael and Taylor, *Far East in the Modern World,* 422–32.

Additional Readings
Clubb, O. Edmund. *Twentieth Century China.* The story of the military course of the war is told on 218–51, with attention also given to political problems.
Johnson, Chalmers A. *Peasant Nationalism and Communist Power: The Emergence of Revolutionary China, 1937–1945.* Stanford: Stanford University Press, 1962. Paperback, 1966. A controversial analysis that attempts to show how the Communists were able to mobilize the peasants and use them for their own purposes as a result of the Japanese invasion. See Selden below.
Selden, Mark. *The Yenan Way in Revolutionary China.* Cambridge: Harvard University Press, 1972. Analysis of reasons for success of Communist policies and programs in mobilizing peasants and other groups for social and economic revolution during Yenan period. See Johnson above.

Discussion Questions
1. Chiang Kai-shek's policy priorities: before the Sino-Japanese War; during the war.
2. The role of the war with Japan in the shifting political fortunes of the KMT; of the CCP.
3. The relative importance of nationalism and of social reform in the shifting fortunes of the CCP.
4. The role of the united-front strategy in the rise of the CCP.

89

XIII. CIVIL WAR, 1945–1949
A. China at the end of World War II
1. Chiang Kai-shek's enhanced national prestige
2. Economic conditions: ravages of war on agriculture and industry; inflation and spectre of hyper-inflation
3. Political conditions: demands for coalition government
4. International relations: relations with USSR; relations with USA; China and the UN
5. Military situation: comparison of Nationalist Army and Red Army—size, territories under control, equipment, morale, and discipline
6. Chiang's estimate of his strength and of domestic situation
7. CCP's estimate of situation
B. Attempts to avert civil war
1. Conferences, negotiations, and the Marshall Mission (1945–46)
2. Insoluble problems: fixing size and control of armies; composition of coalition cabinet
C. Renewal of hostilities and final struggle, 1946–49
1. Race for Manchuria (1945) ; role of USSR and Russian occupation forces
2. Battle for Manchuria (1946–48) ; fall of Mukden
3. Rapid sweep south of Red Army (1948–49) ; fall of Peking
4. Withdrawal of National Government to Taiwan
5. Proclamation of Peoples Republic (Oct. 1, 1949)
D. Significance of Communist victory
1. Reunification of China after century of decentralized authority
2. Commitment to forced modernization
3. Reconstruction of Pacific balance of power

Reading Assignments
Fairbank, *U.S. and China,* 259–82; 304–23.
Fairbank, Reischauer, and Craig, *The Modern Transformation,* 848–60.
Harrison, *China since 1800,* 185–93.
Hsü, *Modern China,* 715–38.
McAleavy, *Modern History of China,* 321–27.

Michael and Taylor, *Far East in the Modern World*, 432–54.
Sources of Chinese Tradition, 877–94; II, 215–32.

Additional Readings
Barnett, A. Doak. *China on the Eve of the Communist Takeover.*
New York: Praeger, 1963. Paperback, 1965. Eyewitness reports on
events and attitudes in China from the years immediately follow-
ing the Sino-Japanese War until the Communist victory.
Feis, Herbert. *The China Tangle: The American Effort in China
from Pearl Harbor to the Marshall Mission.* Princeton: Princeton
University Press, 1953. Atheneum paperback, 1965. A history of
Sino-American relations in this crucial period, with stress on the
American side.
Fitzgerald, C. P. *The Birth of Communist China.* New York: Praeger, 1966. Penguin paperback, 1966. A controversial analysis of
revolution in China in the twentieth century, which argues that
the Communist victory in 1949 followed the pattern of previous
succcessful rebellions throughout Chinese history.
Loh, Pichon, P. Y. *The Kuomintang Debacle of 1949: Conquest or
Collapse?* Boston: D. C. Heath, 1965. A volume in the Problems
of Asian Civilizations series. Excerpts from works giving the full
range of opinions on this highly controversial topic, with a
brief, valuable bibliographical essay.
Tsou, Tang. *America's Failure in China, 1941–1950.* Chicago: University of Chicago Press, 1963. Paperback, in two volumes, 1967.
An analysis of Sino-American relations in the context of the
Chinese civil war and the Kuomintang defeat.

Discussion Questions
1. Compare and contrast Chiang Kai-shek and Mao Tse-tung: background; education; character; analysis of China's problems and
   proposed solutions.
2. Interpretations of the Communist victory in the civil war: a
   victory of superior military organization and power; a political
   victory; poverty of KMT ideology; the only acceptable alterna-
   tive to a demoralized and unpopular KMT; the victory of a
   coalition between scholars and peasants, as in traditional Chinese
   rebellions. The role of foreign powers in the Communist victory.

XIV. COMMUNIST CHINA, 1949-1972
  A. Period of stabilization and early transition, 1949-52
    1. Consolidation of power
      a. Establishment of Government of the People's Republic of China
      b. Pervasiveness of CCP control
        1) Expansion of party membership
        2) Domination of government at all levels
        3) Mass organizations and mobilization of populace
      c. Extension of state and party organization to village level
      d. Thought reform of intellectuals
      e. Party control of the arts
      f. Mass campaigns to create enthusiasm and isolate opposition elements
    2. Steps toward modernization
      a. Social reform
        1) Marriage law and equality of women
        2) Language reform and programs for mass literacy
      b. Economic
        1) Price stabilization
        2) Recovery of production to prewar levels
        3) Land reform: confiscation and redistribution of land
        4) Extensive nationalization of industry, banking, and commerce
    3. Foreign affairs
      a. Treaty of Friendship and Alliance with Soviet Union
      b. Soviet assistance in industrialization program
      c. China and Korean War
  B. First stages of planned industrialization, 1953-57
    1. Political
      a. Proclamation of Constitution; meeting of First National Peoples Congress
      b. Purge within top levels of CCP
      c. Foreign policy of moderation
        1) Era of good feelings among nations: Nehru and "Five Principles of Peaceful Coexistence"; Bandung Conference and "Bandung Spirit" of good will

     2) Mao Tse-tung's assertion of shift in world balance of power in favor of Communist bloc ("east wind prevails over west wind," 1957)

  2. Economic advancement following model of Soviet Russia

    a. First Five Year Plan for economic development (1953–57)

    b. Emphasis on development of heavy industry

    c. Cooperativization of agriculture; Agricultural Producers Cooperatives (APC) ; role of agriculture as principal source of capital investment for industry

  3. Intellectual experimentation

    a. Brief period of freedom of expression; outspoken criticisms of Communist rule (Hundred Flowers Bloom, 1956–57)

    b. Mao's doctrine of nonantagonistic contradictions in society (1957)

C. Great Leap Forward, 1958–60

  1. Headlong industrialization

    a. Agriculture: establishment of Communes through amalgamation of APC's; Communes as an innovation in Marxist theory

    b. Industry: decentralization of authority; planning on provincial level; steel furnaces in Communes

    c. Disruption of economy; lack of coordination; natural disasters

  2. Repercussions of Hundred Flowers period: Anti-Rightist campaign

  3. Revolt in Tibet (1959)

  4. Worsening of Sino-Soviet relations

    a. Ideological differences: impact of de-Stalinization in Russia

    b. Conflicts of national interest

    c. Decline in Soviet aid and withdrawal of Russian technicians

D. Period of recovery and moderate advance, 1961–66

  1. Economic

    a. Reversal of priorities in planning and development (agriculture, light industry, heavy industry)

    b. Division of Communes into smaller units

  2. Foreign affairs

    a. Border clashes with India (1962)

b. Widening rift with Soviet Union

c. Shift to Western world in trade partners

d. First atomic bomb test (1964)

e. China and Third World, successes and failures

f. China and United States in Vietnam

3. Increasing role of army in political affairs

E. Great Proletarian Cultural Revolution, 1966–69

1. Causes: Mao's dissatisfaction with widespread loss of revolutionary spirit and routinism of bureaucracy; power struggles within CCP; frustrations and tensions within society

2. Changes in leadership: fall of Liu Shao-ch'i and other top leaders; rise of Lin Piao

3. Decline of authority of CCP: Red Guard assault on CCP leaders; role of People's Liberation Army; Revolutionary Committees

4. Replacement of material by ideological incentives

5. Decentralization and group decision-making

F. Post Cultural Revolution Stabilization, 1970–

1. Fall of Lin Piao (1971)

2. Foreign relations

a. People's Republic of China enters UN

b. Thaw in US-China relations; President Nixon's trip to China (1972)

G. Problems and prospects

1. Population problem

a. Size and rate of growth of population

b. Implications for economic development

c. Birth control in Communist China

2. Mao Tse-tung and problem of succession

3. Decline of revolutionary spirit and periodic attempts to reinvigorate party and populace; revolutionary fervor vs. efficiency (Red vs. Expert)

4. China as model for developing nations: techniques of guerilla warfare in "semi-colonial" nations; forced industrialization in "newly emerging" nations

5. American policy toward China

Reading Assignments

Fairbank, *U.S. and China*, 324–422.

Fairbank, Reischauer, and Craig, *The Modern Transformation*, 860–84.

Harrison, *China since 1800,* 195–260.
Hsü, *Modern China,* 740–79; 795–99.
McAleavy, *Modern History of China,* 328–65.
Michael and Taylor, *Far East in the Modern World,* 455–515.
Sources of Chinese Tradition, 894–946; II, 232–84.

Additional Readings

Barnett, A. Doak. *Cadres, Bureaucracy, and Political Power in Com-munist China.* New York: Columbia University Press, 1967. A de-tailed description of the organization and operations of a govern-ment ministry, a county, and a commune, based on interviews with *émigrés* from Communist China.
Eckstein, Alexander, et al. (eds.). *Economic Trends in Communist China.* Chicago: Aldine, 1968. Nontechnical surveys of the most important aspects of the Chinese economy by leading authorities.
Klein, Donald W., and Anne B. Clark (eds.). *Biographical Diction-ary of Chinese Communism, 1921–1965.* 2 volumes. Cambridge: Harvard University Press, 1971. Fact-filled biographies of 433 leading Chinese Communists, varying in length according to im-portance. An indispensable reference work.
Schram, Stuart R. *Mao Tse-tung.* New York: Simon and Schuster, 1966. Penguin paperback, 1967. A biography of the Communist leader, which is at the same time an excellent short history of the Chinese Communist Party.
Schram, Stuart R. *The Political Thought of Mao Tse-tung.* Revised edition. New York: Praeger, 1969. Paperback, 1969. The long introduction gives an intellectual biography of Mao that comple-ments the more political biography above. The remainder of this book contains excerpts from Mao's most important writings, with introductory comments by Schram.
Schurmann, Franz. *Ideology and Organization in Communist China.* New, enlarged edition. Berkeley: University of California Press, 1969. Paperback, 1969. A comprehensive and stimulating analysis of important domestic developments, with emphasis on the changing organization of Chinese society. Difficult reading, and not always well balanced in interpretation, yet rewarding.
Schwartz, Benjamin I. *Communism and China: Ideology in Flux.* Cambridge: Harvard University Press, 1968. Atheneum paper-back, 1971. A collection of essays on interrelations between ideology and Chinese domestic and foreign policies by the most perceptive American commentator on Chinese politics.

Two brief paperback introductions to the government and politics of the People's Republic are Franklin W. Houn, *A Short History of Chinese Communism* (Englewood Cliffs, N.J.: Prentice-Hall, 1967), and Derek J. Waller, *The Government and Politics of Communist China* (New York: Doubleday-Anchor, 1971).

Three excellent collections of articles, many of which previously appeared in the leading professional journal on contemporary China, *The China Quarterly*, are A. Doak Barnett (ed.), *Chinese Communist Politics in Action* (Seattle: University of Washington Press, 1969; Paperback, 1969); John Wilson Lewis (ed.), *Party Leadership and Revolutionary Power in China* (Cambridge: Cambridge University Press, 1970; Paperback, 1970); and John M. H. Lindbeck (ed.), *China: Management of a Revolutionary Society* (Seattle: University of Washington Press, 1971; Paperback, 1971).

Discussion Questions

1. Change and continuity in China under the Communists. Similarities in ideas and institutions in traditional China and Communist China. Differentiate between similarities in form and similarities in substance. What is new in Communist China?
2. China's population problem: scope; relation to the problem of modernization; political implications.
3. Nationalism and Marxism as motivations of the Communist leadership; to what extent are Nationalism and Marxism compatible in the Chinese case?
4. The problem of modernization: definition of the term; typical and unique aspects of the problem in China; prospects for the future. Mao Tse-tung's image of the future China; China as model for developing nations.
5. Causes and consequences of the Sino-Soviet dispute; implications for Chinese domestic development.
6. The problem of defining "merit": cf. Red vs. Expert in Communist China and Confucian virtue vs. bureaucratic ability in traditional China.
7. The role of ideology: in determining foreign and domestic policies; in uniting leaders and masses; conjunction with and/or contrary to self-interest

MAPS

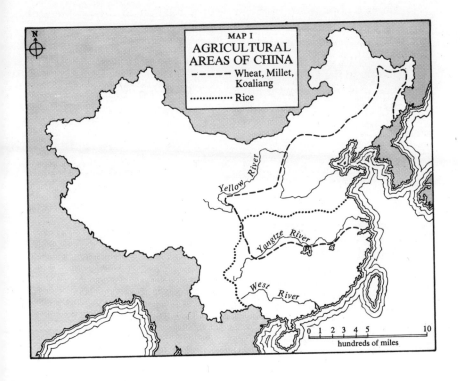

MAP I
AGRICULTURAL AREAS OF CHINA
- - - - - Wheat, Millet, Koaliang
.... Rice

N

Yellow River

Yangtze River

West River

0 1 2 3 4 5   10
hundreds of miles

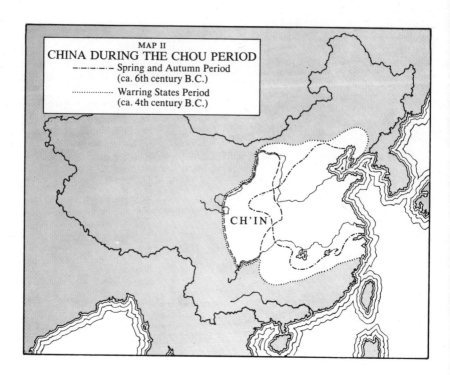

MAP II

CHINA DURING THE CHOU PERIOD

—·—·—·— Spring and Autumn Period
(ca. 6th century B.C.)

················ Warring States Period
(ca. 4th century B.C.)

CH'IN

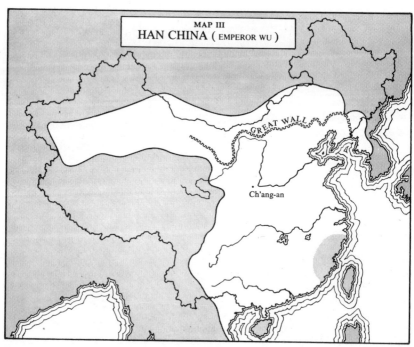

MAP III

HAN CHINA (EMPEROR WU)

GREAT WALL

Ch'ang-an

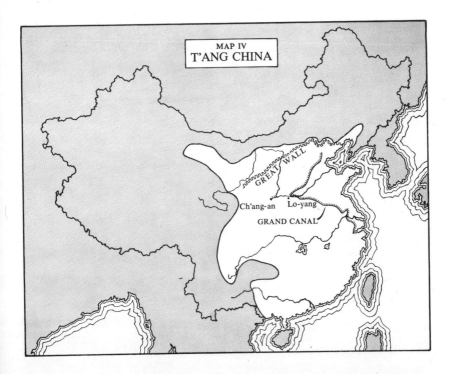

MAP IV
T'ANG CHINA

GREAT WALL

Ch'ang-an   Lo-yang

GRAND CANAL

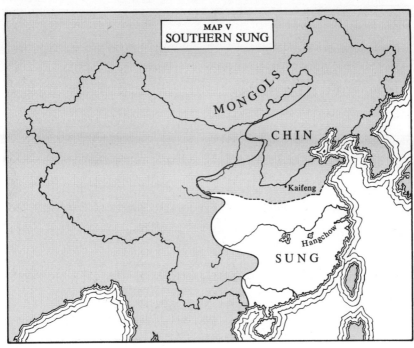

MAP V
SOUTHERN SUNG

MONGOLS

CHIN

Kaifeng

Hangchow

SUNG

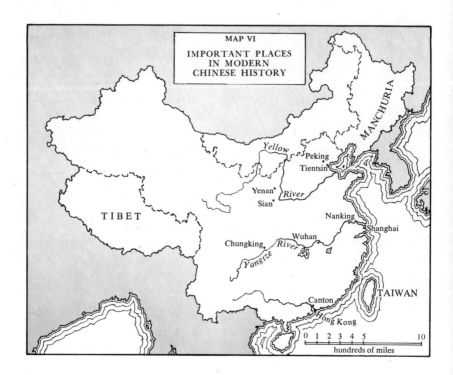

MAP VI

**IMPORTANT PLACES
IN MODERN
CHINESE HISTORY**

MANCHURIA

Yellow
Peking
Tientsin

Yenan•
River
Sian•

TIBET

Nanking
Shanghai

Wuhan
Chungking• *River*

Yangtze

Canton
Hong Kong

TAIWAN

0 1 2 3 4 5   10
hundreds of miles

MAP VII

**THE PROVINCES OF
CONTEMPORARY CHINA**
·········· Autonomous Regions

HEILUNGKIANG

KIRIN

SINKIANG

INNER MONGOLIA

LIAONING

HOPEI

TSINGHAI

KANSU

SHENSI

SHANSI

SHANTUNG

TIBET

HONAN

KIANGSU

ANHWEI

CHEKIANG

SZECHWAN

HUPEI

KWEICHOW

HUNAN

KIANGSI

FUKIEN

YUNNAN

KWANGSI

KWANGTUNG

TAIWAN

0 1 2 3 4 5   10
hundreds of miles

PRONUNCIATION GUIDE TO
MANDARIN CHINESE

The standard system of romanization of Chinese into English is the Wade-Giles system. The following is an attempt to describe how to pronounce Chinese words romanized according to this system. The reader is encouraged to consult other similar attempts as well, such as the explanations in the books listed under Additional Readings in Part One, Section II (p. 8), and in Reischauer and Fairbank, *The Great Tradition*, 675–77.

Vowels

a	as in f*a*ther
e	as *u* in *u*p
i	as *e* in m*e*
o	at the end of a word, usually as *o* in l*o*fty (unless a diphthong, see below)
u	as *oo* in m*oo*
u	when following the double consonants *ss, sz, tz,* or *tz',* muttered as *e* in th*e* in ordinary conversation (for *u* in *u*ng, see below)
ih	as *rrr* in g*rrr;* for instance, *chih* is pronounced as g*er* in passeng*er* (in American English)

Two vowels together are pronounced as diphthongs:

ai	as *i* in r*i*ce
ao	as *ow* in c*ow*
iao	as *iaow* in m*iaow*
ei	as *ay* in d*ay*
ou	as *o* in *o*bey

101

Consonants

The pronunciation of most Chinese consonants is similar to English consonants. A distinction is made between aspirated and unaspirated initial consonants through the use of the ' sign. Aspirated consonants, *ch'*, *k'*, *p'*, *t'*, *ts'*, and *tz'*, are pronounced as *ch*, *k*, *p*, *t*, *ts*, and *tz* in English. Unaspirated consonants, *ch*, *k*, *p*, *t*, *ts*, and *tz*, are pronounced similar to English *j*, *g*, *b*, *d*, *ds*, and *dz*.

There is no difference between the pronunciation of *ts* and of *tz*, or *ts*, and *tz'*. *Tz* and *tz'* are always followed by the single vowel *u*, which is then muttered as the *e* in th*e* in ordinary conversation, so that *tzu* sounds much as *dz* might sound alone, and *tz'u* sounds much as *tz* might sound alone.

j	is pronounced similar to English *r*
hs	is pronounced similar to English *sh,* but lighter
sh	is pronounced as English *sh*
en	is pronounced as *on* in h*on*ey, not as *en* in h*en*
eng	is pronounced as *ung* in h*ung,* not as *eng* in l*eng*th
ien	is pronounced as *yen* (He has a *yen* for ice cream.)
ung	is pronounced *oong,* with *oo* pronounced as in f*oo*t

GLOSSARY OF CHINESE TERMS

CH'I This key term in Neo-Confucian philosophy has been variously translated as matter, material force, vital force, and ether. The earliest meaning of the word seems to have been the spirit or breath that gives life to living things; it also meant the air or ether in the universe. The Neo-Confucians used it in the sense of the basic substance of things, that which gives anything embodiment, as contrasted with *li* (q.v.) .

CHIN-SHIH Presented Scholar, or, more freely, Doctor of Letters. The highest civil service examination in traditional China or a scholar who had passed this examination.

CHÜN Commandary. The provinces of centralizing states during the late Chou and the Han dynasty.

CHÜN-TZU Gentleman, or noble man. The literal meaning of this term, "son of the ruler," is reflected in its meaning of "aristocrat" in the early Chou. From about Confucius' time on, it referred to the ideal man as conceived by the Confucians.

COHONG Authorized Merchant Firm. The Chinese trading firms at Canton that were given monopoly license on trade with Western merchants by the Ch'ing government before the Opium War.

FA Law, method, system, or institution, depending upon the context. The Legalist school takes its name from this term.

HSIEN Prefecture, or county. The lowest level of local government supervised by an official appointed by the central government.

JEN One of the most basic of the Confucian virtues, variously translated as humaneness, humanity, human-heartedness, love, and benevolence.

LI Reason, or principle. A key concept in Neo-Confucianism. The immutable principle underlying all things. The *li* of any genus gives it its essential form. See *ch'i*. (The *li* meaning reason or principle is written with a Chinese character different from the *li* meaning rites, ritual, etc.)

LI Rites, ritual, ceremony, decorum, or propriety. The rules of proper conduct, upon which much stress was laid by the Confucian school. (See *li* above.)

LIKIN Tax of one thousandth. The tax on commerce introduced during the Taiping Rebellion, which remained an important source of revenue for provincial governments into the twentieth century.

PA Hegemon, overlord, or paramount prince. The ruler chosen to be chief among the rulers of states during the early Spring and Autumn period, when the Chou kings had lost authority over these rulers, but still possessed sole legitimate right to the title of King. There were only five hegemons, and the system died out within a hundred years of its inception.

PAO-CHIA The system of mutual responsibility whereby imperial control was extended to the village in traditional China and later in Republican China. In theory, one hundred households formed one *chia,* and ten *chia* made one *pao.*

SHIH At first knight, and later scholar. The class of officials from the lower ranks of the nobility and more humble origins during the Eastern Chou, who rose to prominence and eventually replaced the former ruling aristocracy due to ability rather than hereditary privilege.

TAO Literally, path or way. A key term in Chinese philosophy, used in Taoism (which derives its name from the word), Confucianism, and Buddhism. In Taoism, *Tao* is the way of nature, or of the universe, the ineffable, ultimate first principle, or the basic, undifferentiated unity of everything. In Confucianism, *Tao* signifies the proper way of man, that is, the immutable moral principles that all men should follow. In Buddhism, it refers to the truths of that doctrine.

TSUNGLI YAMEN Office for the General Management of Foreign Affairs, established in Peking in 1861. This office acted as a Foreign Office until the establishment of the Ministry of Foreign Affairs in 1901.

TUCHÜN Military Director, or warlord. The military governors or warlords that controlled regions, small and large, in early Republican China.

WU-WEI Nonaction, nonstriving, or effortlessness. The Taoist doctrine that the proper aim of the sage can be attained through passivity rather than through purposeful action.

GUIDE TO ILLUSTRATIVE
MATERIALS

The *Newsletter* of the Association for Asian Studies, published five times each year, contains a valuable section on "Instructional Programs and Teaching Materials," giving up-to-date information on special lectures, traveling art exhibits, and similar programs in addition to new illustrative materials as these appear. The *Newsletter* is sent to members of the Association. A subscription for nonmembers is available through the Association for Asian Studies, Inc., 1 Lane Hall, University of Michigan, Ann Arbor, Michigan, 48104.

Maps, Atlases, Gazetteers, and Globes
   The following companies and societies all handle reliable maps and similar materials on Asia. Catalogues are available upon request.

American Geographical Society
Broadway at 156th Street
New York, N. Y. 10032

Rand McNally and Company
Education Division
P. O. Box 7600
Chicago, Ill. 60680

Denoyer-Geppert Company
5325 Ravenswood Avenue
Chicago, Ill. 60640

National Geographic Society
16th and M Streets, N. W.
Washington, D. C. 20036

C. C. Hammond and Company
Education Division
515 Valley Street
Maplewood, N. J. 07040

A. J. Nystrom and Company
3333 Elston Avenue
Chicago, Ill. 60618

   The following annotated guides for maps and similar materials are very useful.

105

A Guide to Films, Filmstrips, Maps and Globes, Records on Asia, and the *Supplement* to this guide, both published by The Asia Society, 112 East 64th Street, New York, N. Y., 10021.

L. A. Peter Gosling. *Maps, Atlases and Gazetteers for Asian Studies: A Critical Guide.* Occasional Publication No. 2 of the Foreign Area Materials Center, University of the State of New York, State Education Department. Available for $1.00 from the Foreign Area Materials Center, 33 West 42nd Street, New York, N. Y., 10036.

Theodore Herman. *The Geography of China: A Selected and Annotated Bibliography.* Occasional Publication No. 7 of the Foreign Area Materials Center, University of the State of New York, State Education Department. Available for $2.00 from the Foreign Area Materials Center, 33 West 42nd Street, New York, N. Y., 10036.

Films and Filmstrips

Films and filmstrips on China are available from the following firms, some of which have local distributors throughout the country.

Athena Films, Inc.
165 West 46th Street
New York, N. Y. 10019

Bailey Films, Inc.
De Longpre Avenue
Hollywood, Calif. 90028

Brandon Films, Inc.
200 West 57th Street
New York, N. Y. 10019

China Films
1765 Fulton Street
Palo Alto, Calif. 94303

Chinese News Service
1270 Sixth Avenue
New York, N. Y. 10020

Contemporary Films, Inc.
267 West 25th Street
New York, N. Y. 10001

Educational Film Library
Syracuse University
Syracuse, N. Y. 13210

Encyclopaedia Britannica Films, Inc.
1150 Wilmette Avenue
Wilmette, Ill. 60091

Film Distribution
The Jim Handy Organization
2821 East Grand Boulevard
Detroit, Mich. 48211

Harmon Foundation
Division of Visual Experiment
140 Nassau Street
New York, N. Y. 10038

McGraw-Hill Book Company, Inc.
Text-Film Division
330 West 42nd Street
New York, N. Y. 10036

National Educational Television
Audio-Visual Center
Indiana University
Bloomington, Ind. 47401

New York University Film Library
26 Washington Place
New York, N. Y. 10003

Yeshiva University
Audio-Visual Center
Film Library
526 West 187th Street
New York, N. Y. 10033

World Color Slides
200 Collingsworth Drive
Rochester, N. Y. 14625

In addition, two useful brochures are published by The Asia Society, 112 East 64th Street, New York, N. Y., 10021: *Films on Asia: Select List,* and *A Guide to Films, Filmstrips, Maps and Globes, Records on Asia* (listed above).